NEW CONCEPTS IN TECHNICAL TRADING SYSTEMS

J. WELLES WILDER, JR.

TREND RESEARCH
P.O. BOX 450
GREENSBORO, N.C. 27402

ACKNOWLEDGMENTS

I wish to express sincere appreciation to my associates who have helped to make this book possible.

To Richard C. Meekins who devoted many hours to the perfection of the graphs, work sheets and diagrams presented in the book.

To my "Gal Friday", Carol Lawson, who kept the coffee hot and battled pages of manuscript to the final draft.

Chart in Section VI reprinted by permission of Commodity Perspective, 327 S. LaSalle, Chicago, Illinois 60604.

Printed in the United States of America by Hunter Publishing Company, Winston-Salem, North Carolina.
ISBN 0-89459-027-8
Library of Congress Card Catalog No. 78-60759

All rights reserved. No part of this book may be reproduced in any form whatsoever, by photograph or mimeograph or by any other means, by broadcast or transmission, by translation into any kind of language, nor by recording electronically or otherwise, without permission in writing from the copyright holder, except by a reviewer, who may quote brief passages in critical articles and reviews.

© 1978 by J. Welles Wilder, Jr.

INTRODUCTION

The concepts, methods and systems presented in this book are the result of many years of study and research in the market. The approach is strictly technical and the results are definitive. The purpose of this book is not to entertain, but rather to equip the reader with specific concepts, tools and indexes to use in trading the markets.

Nothing in this book has been taken from a previous author's work. What you are about to read is original. I have tried to present the material in such a way that it will be readily understandable to the beginning trader as well as the seasoned professional who is familiar with systems technology. This is a difficult task. I realize that the beginner may find himself reading through the text several times in order to completely comprehend the material and the computer whiz kids will find the information overly simplified; however, I think the average trader will find the material set out in a way that is reasonably easy to follow.

The programmable calculator, due to its relatively inexpensive cost, is readily becoming an indispensable tool for the technical trader. All of the systems and indexes in this book can be programmed on most of the programmable calculators now on the market. Usually the dealer who sells programmable calculators also has personnel capable of writing programs to be used in the calculator and it should be easy for this person to program your calculator for any or all systems in this book.

Following any of these systems with a programmable calculator is extremely simple. Just punch in the latest price data, push the compute key and the answer will appear either on a register or on a printout in less than a second.

Most programmable calculators also have the capacity to store a particular program and data on a magnetic card; thus, by changing magnetic cards, you can go from one system to another in a matter of a few seconds.

The systems in this book have been programmed for the Hewlett Packard hand-held programmable calculator, HP-41 CV, the Apple II (+ & E) computers and the IBM-PC computer. A brochure is available upon request describing the NEW CONCEPTS software package for each of these computers from Trend Research, Ltd. P.O. Box 128, McLeansville, N.C. 27301. Telephone (919) 698-0500.

DIVISION OF CONCEPTS

This book is divided into ten different sections. The reason for this division is that each section can be studied independently of any previous or following section, except for Section I.

Section I should be read first, as it pertains to certain basic tools and definitions which apply to all following sections. For instance, if your initial interest is in directional movement, you may read Section I first and then skip to Section IV without having to first read Sections II and III.

However, **before beginning to trade** any of these systems, be sure to read Sections IX and X. The Table of Contents classifies the sections as described above.

WORK SHEETS

For each index and system presented in this book, a daily work sheet has been developed to facilitate following the method on a daily basis.

With the exception of the **Relative Strength Index**, which is a chart interpretation technique, all other indexes and systems can be followed using only the daily work sheets. It is not necessary to construct charts, although some traders may want to use charts as visual aids.

At the end of each section, an example of the index or system is worked out using the daily work sheet. If reading through the text does not give you an immediate grasp of the method, then it will all fall into place when you follow the example on the daily work sheet.

A blank copy of each work sheet is provided in the Appendix so it can be reproduced on any standard office copier and used in following the particular system on a daily basis.

CHARTS

Although it is not necessary to construct charts to follow the systems in this book, most technical traders subscribe to a good chart service.

I prefer the COMMODITY PERSPECTIVE charts because each commodity and currency is printed on a separate sheet 13 inches high and 10 inches wide. Ample space is provided after the last price bar to up-date the chart for the following week. These charts are received each Monday morning and are updated through the previous Friday.

An example of the COMMODITY PERSPECTIVE chart is presented with the **Relative Strength Index** in Section VI. If interested in using this type of chart, a subscription is available from:

Investor Publishing, Inc.
327 South La Salle
Chicago, Illinois 60604

PARAMETER RANGES
(An infinite number of systems)

One of the problems in presenting a definitive technical system to a number of traders is the fear of the trader that others are trading the same system, causing a concentration of orders at the exact same point; thereby resulting in bad fills. This problem has been alleviated where possible by giving a range of parameters. Each trader can choose his own parameters and constants to use with the system **within the range given**. The differences in the end result will be insignificant.

For an example of this, suppose that a parameter for a hypothetical system states that a *Long* trade is to be exited on a 30% retracement from a new High to point P. The constant is then .30. In other words, measure the vertical distance from hypothetical point P to the highest point reached while in the *Long* trade. By taking 30% of that distance and subtracting it from the highest point, the stop price is determined.

How did the author of this system determine 30% to be the absolute best distance to use? If he determined the constant using only eight trades on one particular commodity or stock, he would have found that varying the distance just slightly could result in one bad trade and his overall result would be decreased significantly. However, if he determined this constant using 400 trades on each of 20 different commodities, he would have found that the results would be virtually the same if he had used 29% or 31%. There would be very little variation if he had used 28.4% or 31.6%. By using 27% or 33%, he would begin to see a small decrease in the overall profit. By using 20% or 40%, he might see a drastic reduction in his profit.

The results of this hypothetical situation can be compared to a 'bell curve.'

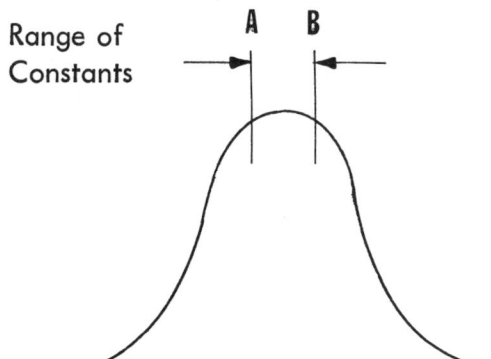

Point A represents the lower end of the range at 28%; Point B represents the higher end of the range at 32%. As long as the trader uses a constant between 28% and 32%, the results over the long run will be about the same.

The 'bell curve' analogy would be applicable to the range of constants given (where possible) for the systems in this book.

TABLE OF CONTENTS

Introduction 2

SECTION I

Basics 7
The Missing Part of Most Trading Plans 8

SECTION II

The Parabolic System 9

SECTION III

The Volatility Index 21
The Volatility System 23

SECTION IV

The Directional Movement Concept 35
The Directional Movement System 47

SECTION V

The Momentum Concept 53
The Trend Balance Point System 54

SECTION VI

The Relative Strength Index 63

SECTION VII

The Reaction Trend System 71

SECTION VIII

The Swing Index 87
The Swing Index System 96

SECTION IX

The Commodity Selection Index 111

SECTION X

Capital Management 116
Conclusion 117

APPENDIX

Glossary of Terms and Abbreviations 118
Printed copies of each work sheet 121

SECTION I

BASICS

BASIC TOOLS

The following bar will quickly be recognized by most traders as that period of time representing one trading day.

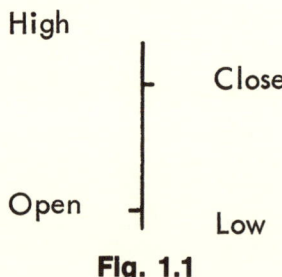

Fig. 1.1

The top of the bar represents the highest price at which the stock or commodity was traded during the day. The low extreme of the bar represents the lowest price at which the stock or commodity was traded during the day. The hash mark on the left side of the bar represents the opening price; the hash mark on the right side represents the closing price.

Reference will be made throughout the book to what is called a LOP and a HIP. LOP is an abbreviation used for LOW POINT. A LOP is any time bar which has a time bar immediately before it, and immediately after it with a higher low.

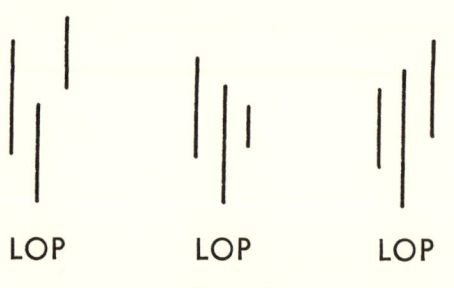

Fig. 1.2

A HIP signifies a HIGH POINT and is defined as any time bar which has a time bar immediately before it, and immediately after it, with a lower high.

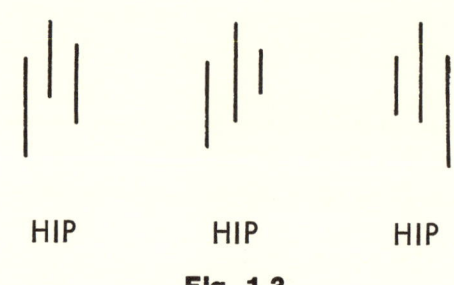

Fig. 1.3

Another configuration which will be used constantly is a SIGNIFICANT POINT which is abbreviated SIP. A SIP must be defined as either a HI SIP or a LO SIP. The HI SIP is defined as being the highest price reached while in a *Long* trade. The LO SIP is defined as the lowest price reached while in a *Short* trade.

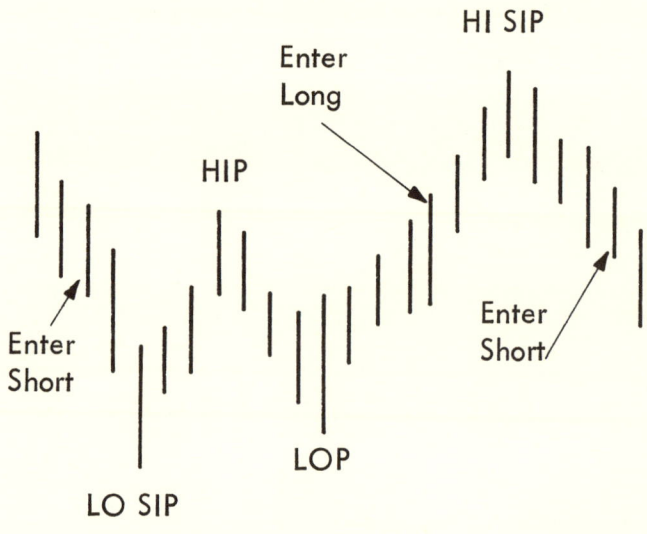

Fig. 1.4

SIC is the abbreviation for SIGNIFICANT CLOSE. The SIC is defined as the extreme favorable CLOSE made while in the trade. If *Long* the SIC is the HIGH SIC which is the highest close made while in the trade. If *Short,* the LOW SIC is the lowest close made while in the trade.

SAR stands for STOP AND REVERSE. This is the point at which a *Long* trade is exited and a *Short* trade is entered, or vice versa. These basic configurations will be referred to repeatedly in the text that follows.

THE MISSING PART OF MOST TECHNICAL TRADING PLANS

Most technical trading plans have two parts:

(1) A technical trading system

(2) A capital management technique

Most technical trading systems are trend-following systems. I believe a trend-following method is the most profitable method to use in trending markets. However, a trend-following method invariably gives back a good part of its profit when the market changes to non-directional sideways movement.

An anti-trend, congestion phase system is profitable in a sideways, non-trending market. However, the profits are smaller, the trades are more frequent and the commissions become a significant factor. When the market changes to a trending mode, the anti-trend system tends to become unprofitable.

In all the years I have spent developing and analyzing technical trading methods, I have yet to see any *one* system that is **consistently** profitable **in all markets**.

The answer then is to devise a rating scale upon which all commodities of interest to the trader can be rated as to whether trending or non-trending. This concept is explained in Section IV entitled THE DIRECTIONAL MOVEMENT INDEX.

There are several other things to consider also. The most profitable trending markets are usually the **volatile** trending markets; that is, the markets that are moving the fastest. This concept is explained in Section III entitled THE VOLATILITY INDEX.

Also, margin requirements and commission charges are factors to be considered.

All four of these factors are **appropriately weighted** and combined in THE COMMODITY SELECTION INDEX (CSI) explained in Section IX. The highest commodities on the CSI scale will be those which:

(1) Are high in directional movement,

(2) Are high in volatility,

(3) Have reasonable margin requirements relative to volatility and directional movement, and

(4) Have reasonable commission rates.

The missing part of most technical trading plans then, is a method for evaluating and determining **which** commodities to trade **when**. The answer presented in this book is THE COMMODITY SELECTION INDEX.

Before we take up some of the heavier concepts such as Directional Movement, Volatility, Momentum, etc., I want to present a relatively simple system which is also very profitable when used in a moving market. It is one of my favorite systems because it squeezes more profit out of an intermediate move (which lasts for two or three weeks) than any method I know. I call it the PARABOLIC TIME/PRICE SYSTEM.

SECTION II

THE PARABOLIC TIME/PRICE SYSTEM

The Parabolic Time/Price System derives its name from the fact that when charted, the pattern formed by the stops resembles a parabola, or if you will, a French Curve. The system allows room for the market to react for the first few days after a trade is initiated and then the stop begins to move more rapidly. The stop is not only a **function of price**, but is also a **function of time**. The stop never backs up. It moves an incremental amount every day, only in the direction in which the trade has been initiated.

For example, if you are *Long*, the stop will move UP every day regardless of the direction the price is moving. This is the TIME function. The stop is also a function of PRICE because the distance the stop moves up is relative to the favorable distance the price has moved . . . specifically, the most favorable price reached since the trade was initiated. This TIME/PRICE concept is most intriguing. In effect, it allows just so much time for the price to move favorably. If the move does not materialize or goes the other way, the stop reverses the position and a new time period begins. This concept is illustrated in the hypothetical illustration. Fig. 2.1.

Notice that the price is moving up exactly the same amount each day. Notice also the pattern formed by the stops. The stop accelerates gradually at first, but then begins to move up rapidly. On the 10th day, the stop is no longer accelerating but becomes a function of price only.

First let's look at the concept of this system by learning how the stops were calculated in the illustration. Let's say that we entered this *Long* trade on Day 4. The stop for the first day in the trade, Day 4, is the SIP. (We have previously defined the SIP as the extreme price point reached while in the previous trade.) Let's assume that our previous trade was *Short* and we are now reversing to *Long* on Day 4. The stop, then, is 50.00 for the day of entry.

This system is a true reversal system; that is, every stop point is also a **reverse point**. We will therefore call each stop point a SAR, which stands for **Stop and Reverse**. On the first day of entry, our SAR is the SIP. We are now ready to calculate the SAR for Day 5.

Take the **highest price** reached on Day 4, subtract from this price the SAR for Day 4 and multiply this distance by the acceleration factor, .02, and then add this amount back to the SAR for Day 4. The result becomes the SAR for Day 5. The equation is as follows:

$SAR_5 = SAR_4 + AF (H_4 - SAR_4)$

Substituting in the above equation:

$SAR_5 = 50.00 + .02 (52.50 - 50.00)$
$SAR_5 = 50.00 + .02 \times 2.50$
$SAR_5 = 50.00 + .05$
$SAR_5 = 50.05$

The SAR for Day 5 then, is 50.05. The ACCELERATION FACTOR (AF) is one of a progression of numbers beginning at .02 and ending at .20. **The AF is increased by .02 each day that a new high is made.** In this example, a new high is made every day; therefore the AF is increased by .02 every day. The SAR for Day 6 would be calculated as follows:

$SAR_6 = SAR_5 + AF (H_5 - SAR_5)$
$SAR_6 = 50.05 + .04 (53.00 - 50.05)$
$SAR_6 = 50.05 + .04 \times 2.95$
$SAR_6 = 50.05 + .12$
$SAR_6 = 50.17$

The general equation, then, is as follows:

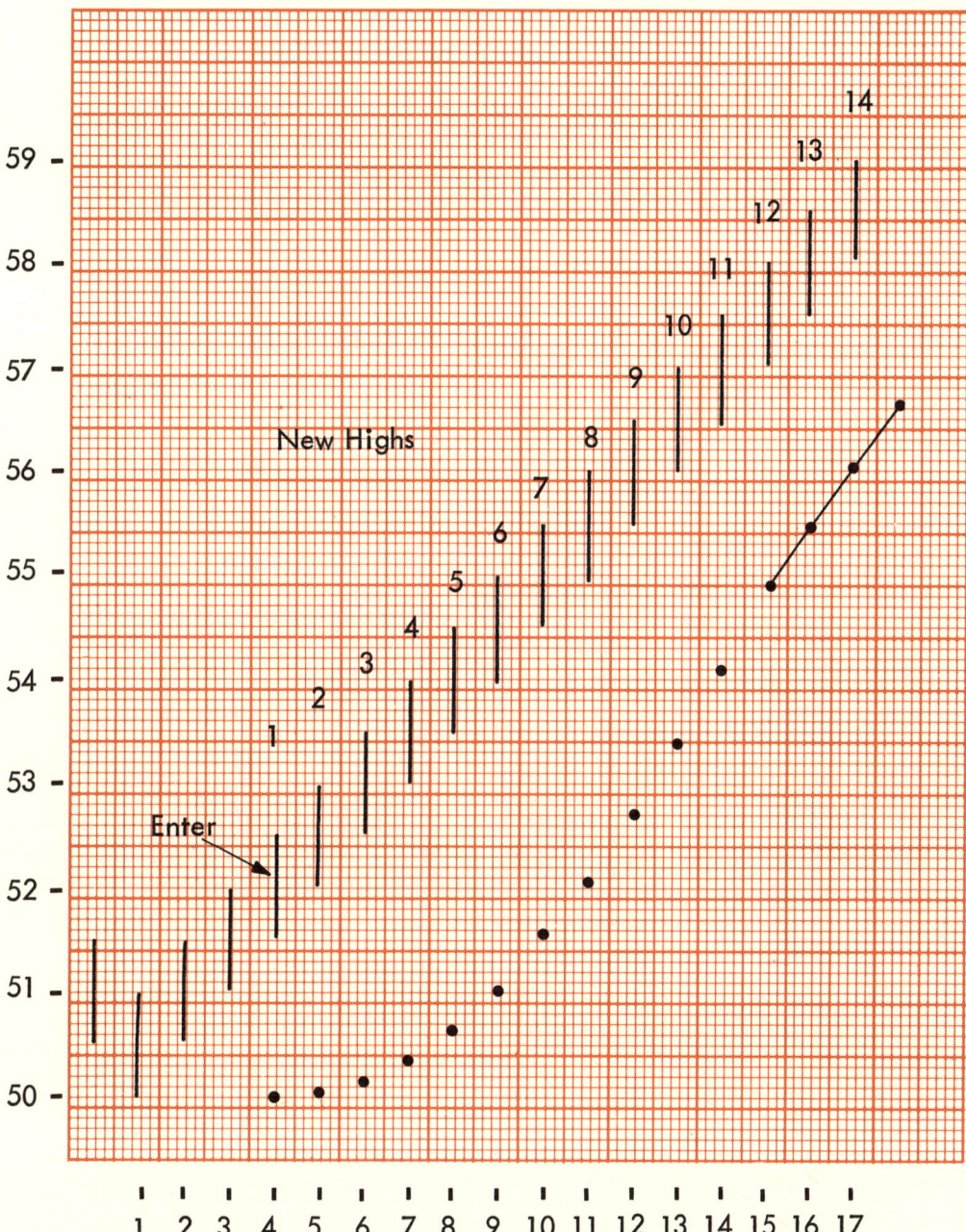

Fig. 2.1

$$SAR_{Tomorrow} = SAR_{Today} + AF(EP_{Trade} - SAR_{Today})$$

Where AF begins at .02 and is increased by .02 until a value of .20 is reached; EP_{Trade} = Extreme Price Point for the trade made so far (If *Long*, EP is the extreme **high** price for the trade; if *Short*, EP is the extreme **low** price for the trade.)

The equations for the SAR for Days 7 through 12 on the chart are as follows:

$SAR_7 = 50.17 + .06(53.50 - 50.17) = 50.37$
$SAR_8 = 50.37 + .08(54.00 - 50.37) = 50.66$
$SAR_9 = 50.66 + .10(54.50 - 50.66) = 51.04$
$SAR_{10} = 51.04 + .12(55.00 - 51.04) = 51.52$
$SAR_{11} = 51.52 + .14(55.50 - 51.52) = 52.08$
$SAR_{12} = 52.08 + .16(56.00 - 52.08) = 52.71$

Now that we understand the concept upon which this system is based, let's state the rules to be used in trading the system.

RULES
PARABOLIC TIME/PRICE SYSTEM

ENTRY:

A position is entered when a price penetrates the SAR.

STOP AND REVERSE (SAR):

A. For the first day of entry, the SAR is the previous SIP (Significant Point).

   1. If entered *Long* the SIP is the **lowest** price reached while in the previous *Short* trade.

   2. If entered *Short,* the SIP is the **highest** price reached while in the previous *Long* trade.

B. For the second day and thereafter, the SAR is calculated as follows:

   1. If *Long:*

      a. Find the difference between the highest price made while in the trade and the SAR for today. Multiply the difference by the AF and **add** the result to the SAR today to obtain the SAR for tomorrow.
      b. Use .02 for the first AF and increase its value by .02 on every day that a **new high** for the trade is made. If a new high is not made, continue to use the AF as last increased. DO NOT INCREASE THE AF ABOVE .20.

   2. If *Short:*

      a. Find the difference between the lowest price made while in the trade and the SAR for today. Multiply the difference by the AF and **subtract** the result from the SAR today to obtain the SAR for tomorrow.
      b. Use .02 for the first AF and increase its value by .02 on every day that a **new low** for the trade is made. If a new low is not made, continue to use the AF as last increased. DO NOT INCREASE THE AF ABOVE .20.

C. Never move the SAR into the previous day's range or today's range.

   1. If *Long,* never move the SAR for tomorrow above the **previous day's low or today's low.** If the SAR is calculated to be above the previous day's low or today's low, then **use the lower low** between today and the previous day as the new SAR. Make the next day's calculations based upon this SAR.

   2. If *Short,* never move the SAR for tomorrow below the **previous day's high or today's high.** If the SAR is calculated to be below the previous day's high or today's high, then **use the higher high** between today and the previous day as the new SAR. Make the next day's calculations based upon this SAR.

Now let's look at a hypothetical example on the work sheet which is illustrated on the following chart Fig. 2.2. For this example, we will assume that we were reversed from a *Short* position to a *Long* position on Day 4. On the initial day of entry, we can give our broker the SAR without making any calculations because we know the **lowest point** reached while in **the previous *Short* trade** was 50.00 (which was the LOW SIP). We are now ready to calculate the SAR for the following day.

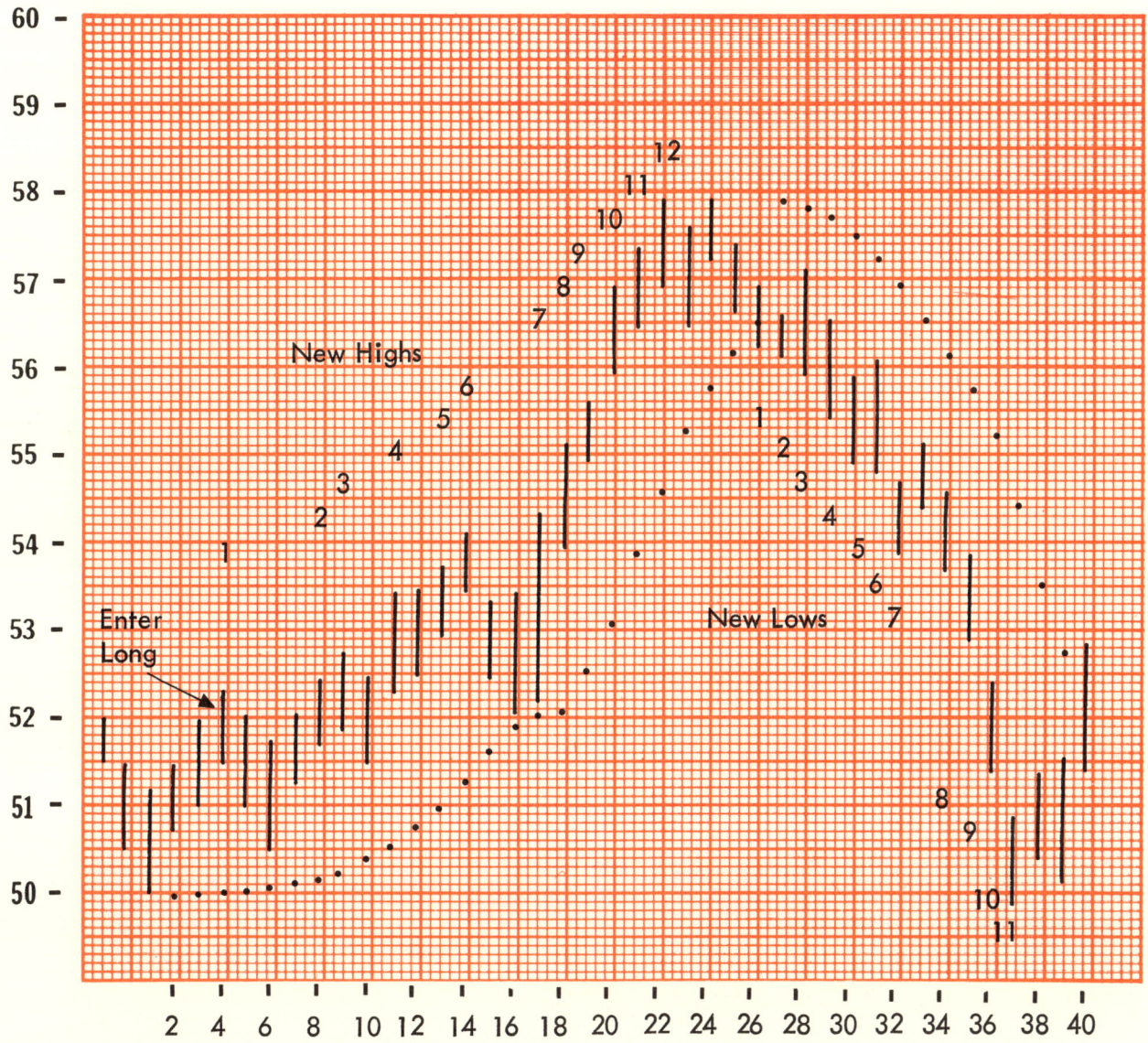

Fig. 2.2

On the worksheet, we have filled out only the High and Low columns for simplicity. In actually following the system, you would want to fill in the Open and Close columns also.

On Day 4, we insert the high of 52.35 and the low of 51.50. Under Column #1, we insert the SAR for today, which, for the first day in the trade is always the previous SIP, so we put 50.00 in Column #1.

Our Extreme Price for the first day in the trade is the high made during that day, and we put 52.35 in Column #2 under EP (Extreme Price.) We then take the difference between 50.00

DAILY WORK SHEET

PARABOLIC TIME / PRICE SYSTEM

DATE	OPEN	HIGH	LOW	CLOSE	(1) SAR	(2) EP	(3) EP±SAR	(4) AF	(5) AF X DIF
4		52.35	51.50		50.00	52.35	2.35	.02	.05
5		52.10	51.00		50.05	52.35	2.30	.02	.05
6		51.80	50.50		50.10	52.35	2.25	.02	.05
					50.15				
7		52.10	51.25			52.35	2.20	.02	.04
8		(52.50)	51.70		50.19	52.50	2.31	.04	.09
9		(52.80)	51.85		50.28	52.80	2.52	.06	.15
					50.43				
10		52.50	51.50			52.80	2.37	.06	.14
11		(53.50)	52.30		50.57	53.50	2.93	.08	.23
12		53.50	52.50		50.80	53.50	2.70	.08	.22
13		(53.80)	53.00		51.02	53.80	2.78	.10	.28
14		(54.20)	53.50		51.30	54.20	2.90	.12	.35
15		53.40	52.50		51.67	54.20	2.55	.12	.31
16		53.50	52.10		51.96	54.20	2.24	.12	.27
17		(54.40)	53.00		52.10	54.40	2.30	.14	.32
18		(55.20)	54.00		52.10	55.20	3.10	.16	.50
19		(55.70)	55.00		52.60	55.70	3.10	.18	.56
20		(57.00)	56.00		53.16	57.00	3.84	.20	.77
21		(57.50)	56.50		53.93	57.50	3.57	.20	.71
22		(58.00)	57.00		54.64	58.00	3.36	.20	.67
23		57.70	56.50		55.31	58.00	2.69	.20	.54
24		58.00	57.30		55.85	58.00	2.15	.20	.43
25		57.50	56.70		56.28	58.00	1.72	.20	.34
					56.62				
26		57.00	(56.30)		58.00	56.30	1.70	.02	.03
27		56.70	(56.20)		57.97	56.20	1.77	.04	.07
28		57.50	(56.00)		57.90	56.00	1.90	.06	.11
29		56.70	(55.50)		57.79	55.50	2.29	.08	.18
30		56.00	(55.00)		57.61	55.00	2.61	.10	.26
31		56.20	(54.90)		57.35	54.90	2.45	.12	.29
32		54.80	(54.00)		57.06	54.00	3.06	.14	.43
33		55.60	54.50		56.63	54.00	2.63	.14	.37
34		54.70	(53.80)		56.26	53.80	2.46	.16	.39
35		54.00	(53.00)		55.87	53.00	2.87	.18	.52
36		52.50	(51.50)		55.35	51.50	3.85	.20	.77
37		51.00	(50.00)		54.58	50.00	4.58	.20	.92
38		51.50	50.50		53.66	50.00	3.66	.20	.73
39		51.70	50.20		52.93	50.00	2.93	.20	.59
		53.00	51.50		52.34				

COMMODITY _____ CONTRACT MONTH _____

NTRY	EXIT	P&L	ACTION and ORDER
52.20			
56.62	56.62	+4.42	
52.35	52.35	+4.27	

14

and 52.35 (i.e., the difference between Column #1 and Column #2) and insert this value, 2.35, in Column #3.

Our first acceleration factor is always .02 and we insert this in Column #4. We now multiply .02 times the difference, 2.35 (Column #3) and obtain .05 to place in Column #5.

Now we are ready to calculate the SAR for tomorrow. Add Column #5 to Column #1 and obtain 50.05. Put this number in Column #1 for the **next day**. This is the SAR for Day 5. Now let's see what happened on Day 5.

The high was 52.10, and the low was 51.00. A **new high was not made for the trade**, so we continue to use the same AF, which is .02. Notice in Column #2, we always put the Extreme Price which, so far, is 52.35. We take the difference between Column #1 and Column #2 and insert 2.30 in Column #3. Multiply Column #3 by Column #4 and obtain .05. We then add this to the SAR for the day, 50.05, and obtain 50.10 as the SAR for tomorrow, Day 6.

Now let's skip to Day 8. On this day, we have a new high of 52.50. We therefore increase our AF for that day by .02 and insert the new AF, .04, in Column #4. We take the extreme high price for the trade, EP, which is 52.50, and subtract our SAR for that day, 50.19. We multiply the difference, 2.31 by .04 and obtain .09. We add this to 50.19 and obtain the SAR for tomorrow, 50.28.

Now skip to Day 16 and let's calculate the SAR for Day 17. The high is 53.50 and the low is 52.10. We take the difference between the EP, 54.20 and the SAR, 51.96 and obtain 2.24. We multiply 2.24 times the AF of .12 and get .27. Add .27 to the SAR of 51.96 and we get 52.23. **However, the low for Day 16 is 52.10.** Since we cannot move the SAR for tomorrow into yesterday's range or today's range, we must back up the SAR to **today's low** which is 52.10. We put 52.10 in Column #1 and use this SAR for tomorrow's calculations.

On the following day, Day 17, we must still hold the SAR at 52.10 because we cannot move the SAR higher than either today's range or yesterday's range.

Every day that we have a **new high**, we will increase the AF by .02 until we get to an AF of .20, at which point we stop increasing the AF. No matter how many new highs are made thereafter, we do not increase the Acceleration Factor beyond .20. Notice on Day 20 the AF reaches .20 which is maintained for the duration of the trade.

Now let's look at what happens when we are reversed to *Short*. On Day 26, our SAR is penetrated and we reverse to *Short* at 56.62. We know that on the day we are reversed, our SAR is the previous HIGH SIP which is the **highest point** reached while in the *Long* trade.

On Day 26, we write down our high of 57.00 and low of 56.30. Under Column #1, we put our SIP which is 58.00. Now, since we are *Short*, we are looking for the **Extreme Low Price** (EP) while in the *Short* trade. For the first day, the EP would be the **low** for the day, so we put 56.30 in Column #2. As before, we take the difference between Column #1 and Column #2 and insert this value, 1.70, in Column #3. We now **start over again** with the AF at .02. Multiply .02 times the difference, which is 1.70, and obtain .03. We now **subtract** .03 from our SAR for today, 58.00 and obtain a SAR for tomorrow of 57.97.

On Day 27, we have a new low for the trade, 56.20. We take the difference between this EP, which we enter in Column #2, and the previous SAR of 57.97 and obtain 1.77. This is the second new low for the trade, so our AF has now jumped to .04. We multiply .04 times 1.77 and obtain .07. We then **subtract** .07 from our SAR that day of 57.97 and obtain a SAR for tomorrow of 57.90. Again, we never increase our AF beyond .20.

One last thing to consider . . . where do we begin trading in this system. Since each entry point is a reverse from a previous trade, where does the first trade start?

If the market is in a general UP trend, go back several weeks to a HI SIP on your chart and make a paper trade *Short* entry on the most significant down day **within** three or four days after the HI SIP. Follow this trade on the chart until you are reversed to a *Long* trade. Make the first market entry at this point, which will usually be in the direction of the general trend.

If the market is in a general DOWN trend, then pick the LO SIP several weeks back and follow the same procedure as above for a *Long* paper trade so that your first market entry will be the next *Short* trade in the direction of the trend.

An alternate way to trade this system is in accordance with the DIRECTIONAL MOVEMENT INDEX explained in Section IV. If directional movement is UP, take only the *Long* trades. If directional movement is DOWN, take only the *Short* trades.

In essence, that is the system. It is very simple to calculate the SAR (stop and reverse point) and it is very easy to follow. Notice that the number used for the AF is always the number of **new highs** (or **new lows**, if *Short*) multiplied by two. For instance, on the sixth new high, the Acceleration Factor is .12; on the eighth new high, the AF is .16, etc.

Although this system is very simple, it is an extremely profitable system in a moving market. Technicians have spent many hours devising moving average systems which would make allowance for reactions at the beginning of the move but would accelerate as the move began to top out. **This system does just that.** By moving the initial stop back to the SIP when a trade is initiated, the system prevents being whipsawed until the price begins to move directionally.

Study the following charts and you will get a good feel for the way this system handles a volatile market. Notice especially the pattern made by the SARs.

I have tried many different acceleration factors on this system and have found that a consistent increase of .02 works best overall; however, if you desire to individualize this system in order to vary the stop points from what others may be using, the range for the incremental increase is between .018 and .021. Any constant increase within this range will work well. Use the number of increases it takes to reach at least .20, but do not exceed .22.

This system should be used primarily in a directional market which can be determined by using THE DIRECTIONAL MOVEMENT INDEX or THE COMMODITY SELECTION INDEX explained in other sections in the book.

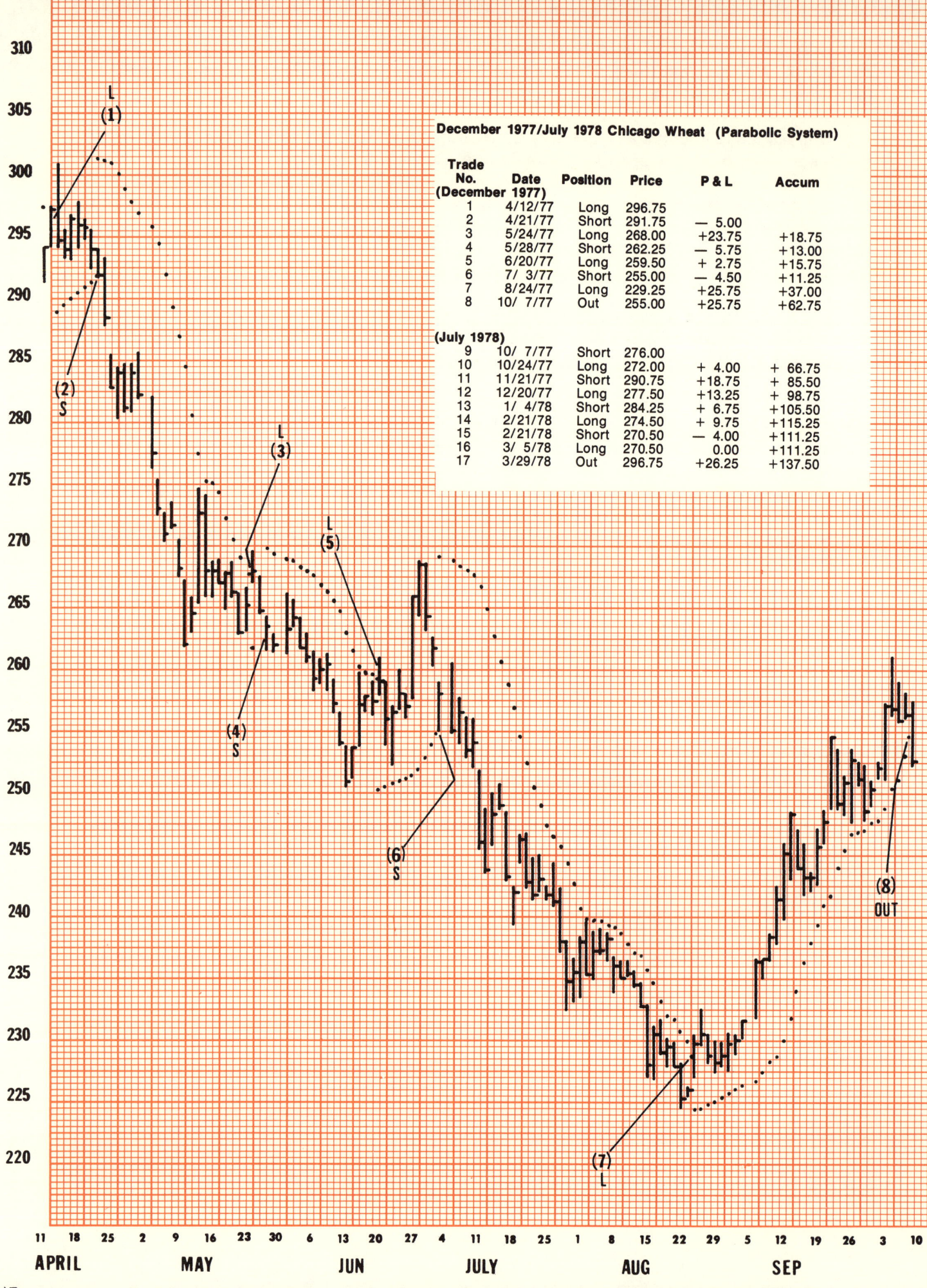

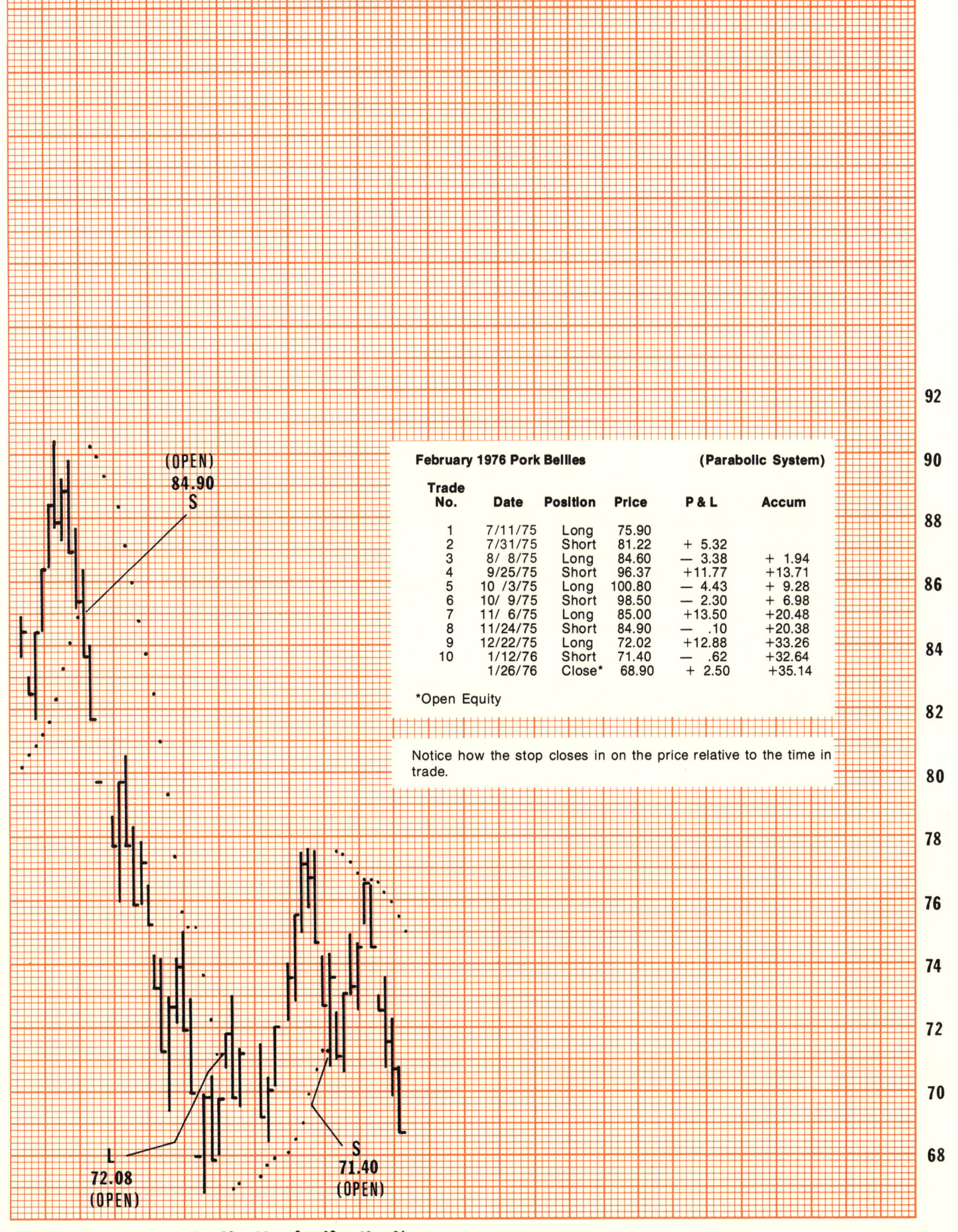

SECTION III

VOLATILITY

THE VOLATILITY INDEX

What is volatility? Most traders will define volatility in terms of market action. If a market is very active, it is volatile. If a market is inactive, it is considered non-volatile. It is easy enough to look at a chart and point out a very volatile market or a very non-volatile market, but how does the trader get a handle on volatility? How can volatility be defined?

The one thing that is directly proportional to volatility is **range**. Range can be defined as the distance the price moves per increment of time.

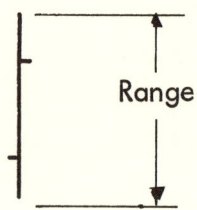

Fig. 3.1

In the time bar Fig. 3.1, it is obvious that the range is simply the distance from the highest point to the lowest point of the bar.

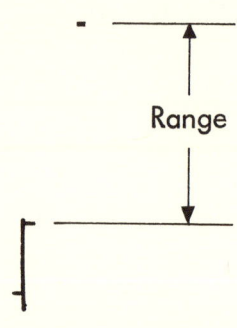

Fig. 3.2

Suppose, however, that as in time bar Fig. 3.2, the price is limit; i.e., either limit up or limit down. In this case, all trades for the day, if any, were made at one price. Would the range then, for a limit day, be zero? Obviously not. If the price has moved as far as it can move in a time period, it certainly would not have a value of zero. The real price range is, in this case, the distance from the previous close to the limit price. By using this distance, we have given the range for time bar Fig. 3.2 the largest value it could have, which is appropriate. It follows then, that the TRUE RANGE to use in describing volatility is the maximum range that the price moved — either during the day or from yesterday's close to the extreme point reached during the day. Therefore, the TRUE RANGE is defined as the **greatest** of the following:

(1) The distance from today's high to today's low.
(2) The distance from yesterday's close to today's high, or
(3) The distance from yesterday's close to today's low.

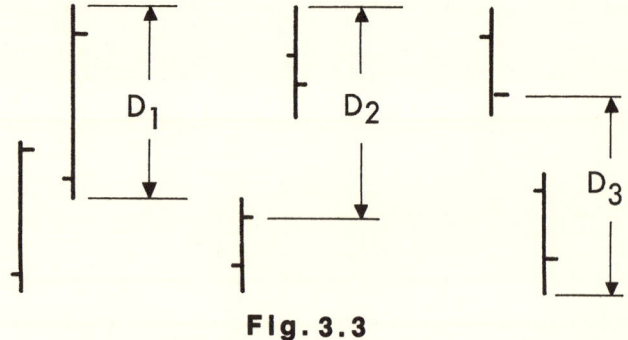

Fig. 3.3

In order for range to be a meaningful tool as a measure of volatility, more than one day's range must be considered. The answer is to consider an **average** of the true range **made per day** over a number of days. A volatility indicator will be fast or slow, depending on the number of days used to obtain the average daily true range. How many days should be used to obtain the average daily true range? After extensive testing, I have found that about 14 days gives the best indicator of volatility to use for the VOLATILITY INDEX.

The VOLATILITY INDEX (VI) is used along with the Directional Movement Index to compute the Commodity Selection Index.

The equation for the VOLATILITY INDEX is:

$$VI_{Today} = \frac{13 \times VI_{Previous} + TR_1}{14}$$

Where TR_1 is today's true range

The numerator in this equation is also used in the Directional Movement Index and the same equation with different constants is explained in the Volatility System which follows.

In the Volatility System, we use a seven day true range average (rather than a 14-day true range average) because this system needs a faster acting average true range than the Volatility Index. The procedure for solving this equation is the same regardless of the number of days used for the average. We will therefore explain in detail the procedure for solving the seven day equation in the next chapter.

THE VOLATILITY SYSTEM

The Volatility System is a trend-following system. It is also a true reversal system which means that the position is reversed at every stop. This system is extremely simple to follow.

Before we discuss the mechanics of the Volatility System, we must learn to calculate the AVERAGE TRUE RANGE. The ATR is the basic unit of measurement for the system. The ATR is based upon seven day's TRUE ranges. We learned how to obtain the TRUE RANGE for one day (TR_1) in the previous chapter. We will now learn how to calculate the AVERAGE TRUE RANGE (ATR.)

The equation for the AVERAGE TRUE RANGE is as follows:

$$ATR_{Latest} = \frac{6 \times ATR_{previous} + \text{Today's True Range}}{7}$$

or

$$ATR_L = \frac{6 \times ATR_p + TR_1}{7}$$

To get the ATR **Initially**, add the true range, as defined, for the past seven days and divide by seven. The answer from this will be used as the ATR_p in the equation for the next day. The following table will illustrate how to calculate the ATR on a daily basis:

Table 3.4

Date	Open	High	Low	Close	Range	ATR	
1/1	50.00	51.20	49.80	50.90	1.40		high to low
1/2	50.70	51.80	50.30	51.50	1.50		high to low
1/3	51.70	52.90	51.70	52.80	1.40		close to high
1/4	52.50	53.70	52.30	53.50	1.40	10.00	high to low
1/5	53.60	54.80	53.50	54.70	1.30	7 = 1.43	high to low
1/6	54.40	54.40	52.90	53.00	1.80		close to low
1/7	52.90	53.20	52.00	52.00	1.20	1.43	high to low
1/8	52.00	52.70	52.00	52.20	.70	1.33	high to low

Starting **Initially,** we add the True Ranges for the first seven days and obtain a total of 10.00.

9.90 ÷ 7 = 1.43 which is the ATR for day 1/7

From now on, we use the ATR equation:

$$ATR_L = \frac{6 \times ATR_p + TR_1}{7}$$

At the end of Day 1/8, the previous ATR is 1.41; therefore:

$$ATR_L = \frac{6 \times 1.43 + .70}{7} = \frac{8.58 + .70}{7} = 1.33$$

Now let's review the procedure for calculating the ATR (Average True Range) on a daily basis. Initially, the ATR is obtained by taking the sum of the ranges for the first seven days and dividing this entire quantity by seven. This gives the ATR for the seventh day. For the eighth day; and thereafter, simply use the ATR for the previous day, multiply it by six, add the true range for the latest day and divide this quantity by seven. By obtaining the ATR is this manner, we only have to keep up with data for the previous day.

Now that we know how to obtain the ATR, there is one thing left to do to make this quantity usable in the Volatility System, and this is to multiply the ATR by a constant (C).

I have found that the multiplier that works best is about 3.0. The range for this constant is 2.8 to 3.1. If you wish to individualize this system (as set out in the Introduction) any constant within this range will work quite well. By multiplying this constant, 3.00, times the ATR, we obtain a number which we will call the ARC (Average Range times Constant). Note that the ARC is directly proportional to the ATR and therefore is directly proportional to volatility. As volatility increases, the ARC increases, and as volatility decreases, the ARC decreases.

In Table 3.4, the open price was listed with the high, low and close prices; however, it was not used in any of the calculations. In following the system on a daily basis, it will be helpful to tabulate the open price which may be pertinent in the case of a gap opening.

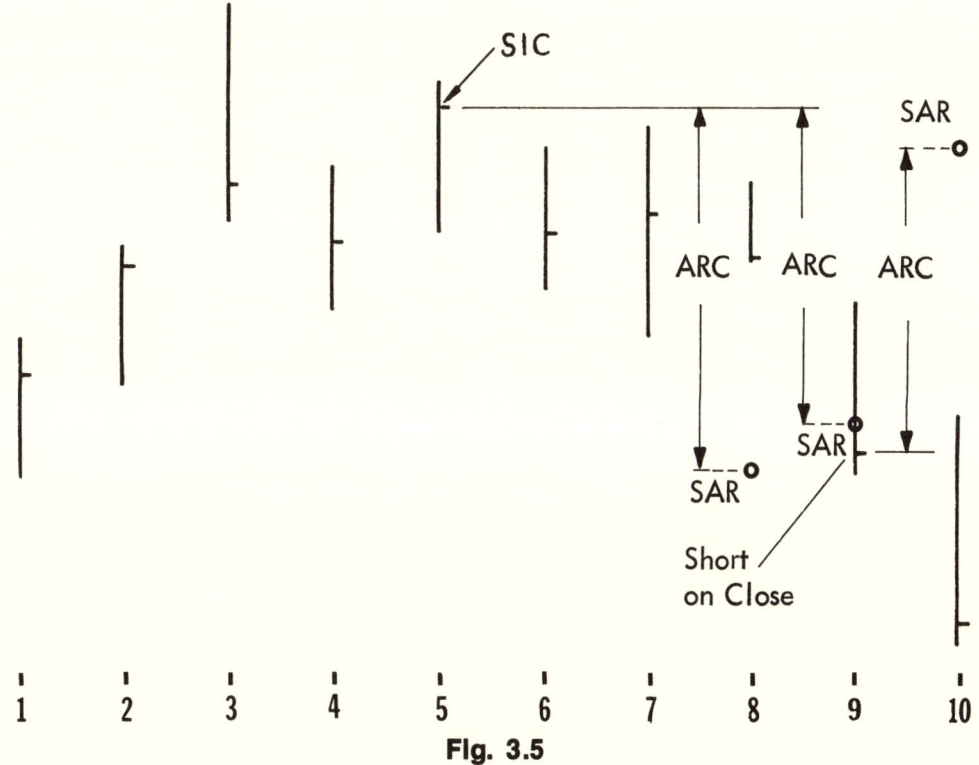

Fig. 3.5

Now let's define the Volatility System:
A position is exited and reversed at a distance of one ARC from the SIC (extreme favorable CLOSE reached while in a trade.)

In Fig. 3.5, the price is going up and making new highs almost every day. We obtain for the previous seven days, the high, low and close prices for the particular contract we want to follow. With this information, the ARC is calculated for the seventh day. Next we take the high CLOSE for the seven day period, the SIC, and **subtract** from it the numerical value of the ARC for that day. This will be the SAR (Stop and Reverse point) to use for the **eighth** day. Let's say that on the ninth day, the price retraces and closes below the SAR, reversing us to a *Short* position. We **add** the ARC distance to the close price (as it is the lowest close since entering the trade) and obtain the SAR for the *Short* trade for the tenth day.

Now let's assume that the *Short* trade moves in our favor and the price continues to go down. We continue to use the ARC distance from the **lowest close** made while in the trade as the SAR until we are stopped and reversed on the first close **above** the ARC distance point (SAR).

Suppose the volatility increases and we are not stopped out of the trade. The ARC distance could increase more than the previous day's ARC distance and push the stop further away from the price. This is okay — when the volatility increases, the system automatically compensates and pushes the stop further away from the extreme favorable close point. This is the nice thing about this system — it is relative both to the extreme close price reached while in the trade and also relative to volatility. If the price becomes very volatile, the SAR compensates by lengthening relative to the increased volatility, yet it remains a function of the most extreme close price reached while in the trade. Conversely, when the market cools down, the volatility decreases and the stop moves closer to the trading price.

To continue with the *Short* trade, let's say the price moves favorably for two or three weeks and then closes above the ARC distance SAR. The new SAR for the *Long* position for the next day is then the ARC distance below the most favorable close . . . in this case, the close at which we reversed.

In trading this system on a daily basis, it is not necessary to draw charts. All the information needed is on the work sheet. I find it helpful to put parenthesis around the Significant Closes (SICs) as a point of reference.

That's all there is to the VOLATILITY SYSTEM. However, don't let the simplicity of the system fool you. The key point, which is the SAR (Stop and Reverse) is relative to the extreme close price and also relative to volatility. It compensates automatically when the price slows down or speeds up. The Constant, C, multiplier of the Average True Range, ATR, is gauged to keep the trader in the trade as long as the trend is intact. It allows for retracements or reactions but it is also gauged to reverse the position when the price has reacted enough to indicate a change in direction of the major trend. If the trend should resume in the same direction, the trader is automatically reversed at the ARC SAR and put right back in the direction of the trend.

Following are the rules set out for quick reference. An example worked out on the work sheet and a corresponding chart are also included. By following the work sheet and chart, a complete understanding of the system should be grasped very quickly.

THE VOLATILITY SYSTEM

DEFINITIONS:

1. TRUE RANGE is the greatest of the following:
   A. Today's high to today's low,
   B. Today's high to yesterday's close, or
   C. Today's low to yesterday's close.

2. ATR — AVERAGE TRUE RANGE
   A. Initially obtained by adding the true ranges for seven days and dividing by seven.
   B. The latest ATR is obtained by multiplying the previous ATR by six, adding today's true range and then dividing the total by seven.

3. C — CONSTANT Any number between 2.80 and 3.10.

4. ARC — The ATR multiplied by the Constant C.

5. SIC — The Significant Close; the extreme favorable close price reached while in a trade.

6. SAR — The Stop and Reverse point; a point defined by the ARC distance from the SIC.

RULES

1. **ENTRY** is made on the Close when the price closes contrary to the SAR.

2. **STOP AND REVERSE (SAR)**
   A. From *Long* to *Short:* on the Close when the close is below the ARC distance point from the highest close made while in the trade. That is, when the close is **below** the SAR.
   B. From *Short* to *Long:* On the Close when the close is above the ARC distance point from the lowest close made while in the trade. That is, when the close is **above** the SAR.

DAILY WORK SHEET
VOLATILITY SYSTEM

COMMODITY _____   **CONTRACT MONTH** _____

DATE	OPEN	HIGH	LOW	CLOSE	TR$_1$	ATR	ARC	SAR	ACTION and ORDER
1	52.80	53.00	52.50	52.70	.50				
2	52.60	52.75	52.25	52.55	.50				
3	52.00	52.35	51.85	(52.30)	.70	4.05 ÷ 7 = .58			
4	52.20	52.45	52.15	52.40	.30				
5	52.10	52.35	51.75	51.90	.65				
6	51.90	52.10	51.50	51.65	.60				
7	51.50	51.80	51.00	(51.10)	.80	.58	1.74		
8	51.15	51.60	51.25	51.55	.50	.57	1.71	52.84	
9	51.50	51.70	51.40	51.65	.30	.53	1.59	52.81	
10	51.60	51.60	51.10	51.15	.55	.53	1.59	52.69	
11	51.00	51.40	50.75	(50.75)	.65	.55	1.65	52.69	
12	51.35	51.75	51.35	51.65	1.00	.61	1.83	52.40	
13	51.70	51.90	51.40	51.80	.50	.59	1.77	52.58	
14	51.60	51.70	51.15	51.55	.65	.60	1.80	52.52	
15	51.55	51.80	51.50	51.80	.30	.56	1.68	52.53	
16	51.90	52.50	51.80	52.50	.70	.58	1.74	52.43	L-52.50
17	52.40	52.70	52.10	(52.70)	.60	.58	1.74	50.76	
18	52.20	52.45	52.00	52.10	.70	.60	1.80	50.96	
19	52.00	52.65	51.50	52.65	1.15	.68	2.04	50.90	
20	52.50	52.95	52.40	52.90	.55	.66	1.98	50.66	
21	53.10	53.60	53.05	53.55	.70	.67	2.01	50.92	
22	53.95	54.50	53.80	54.50	.95	.71	2.13	51.54	
23	55.20	55.70	55.00	56.55	1.20	.78	2.34	52.37	
24	57.55	57.55	57.55	57.55	2.00	.95	2.85	53.21	
25	57.90	58.55	57.90	(58.55)	1.00	.96	2.88	54.70	
26	57.75	57.75	57.30	57.65	1.25	1.00	3.00	55.67	
27	57.50	58.05	57.15	57.95	.90	.99	2.97	55.53	
28	57.80	57.90	57.45	57.80	.50	.92	2.76	55.58	
29	58.00	58.30	57.85	58.20	.50	.86	2.85	55.79	
30	58.45	58.65	57.75	58.65	.90	.87	2.61	55.97	
31	57.80	57.80	57.00	57.30	1.65	.98	2.94	56.04	
32	57.00	57.15	56.25	56.60	1.05	.99	2.97	55.71	
33	56.30	56.35	55.35	56.30	1.25	1.03	3.09	55.68	
34	56.20	56.60	56.05	56.60	.55	.96	2.88	55.56	
35	56.50	57.25	56.40	57.25	.85	.94	2.82	55.77	
36	57.25	57.50	57.00	57.50	.50	.88	2.64	55.83	
37	57.50	57.50	57.25	57.25	.25	.79	2.37	56.01	
38	57.00	57.15	56.50	56.60	.75	.78	2.34	56.28	
39	56.50	56.60	56.25	56.45	.35	.72	2.16	56.31	
40	56.50	56.90	56.45	56.90	.45	.68	2.04	56.49	
41	57.00	57.25	56.75	57.10	.50	.65	1.95	56.61	
42	57.40	57.60	57.00	57.40	.60	.64	1.92	56.70	
43	57.20	57.25	56.90	57.05	.50	.62	1.86	56.73	
44	57.25	58.00	57.25	57.90	.95	.67	2.01	56.79	
45	58.00	58.50	57.00	57.00	1.50	.79	2.37	56.64	
46	56.50	56.50	55.50	56.05	1.50	.89	2.67	56.22	S-56.05
47	56.00	56.35	55.75	55.85	.60	.85	2.55	58.72	
								58.40	

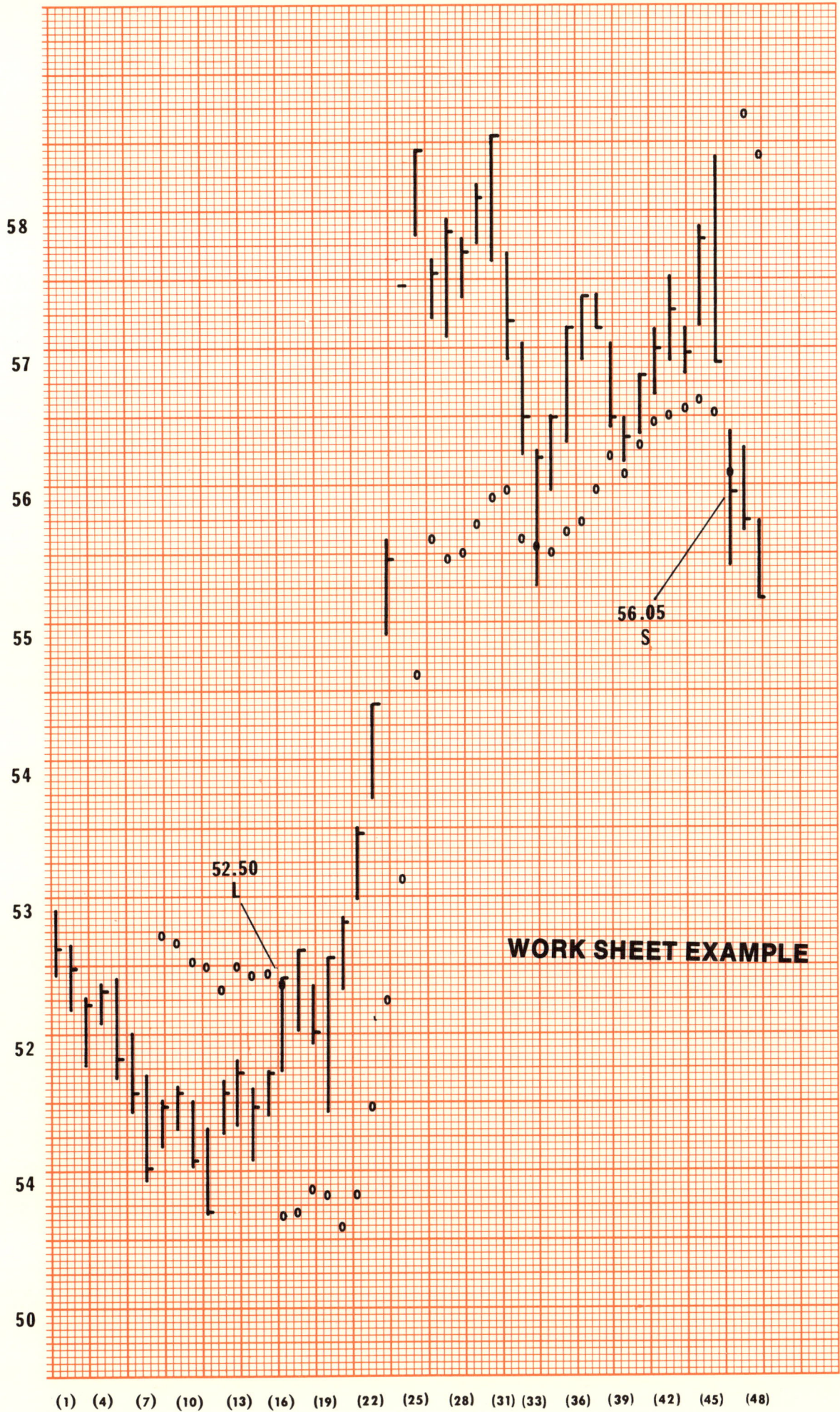

WORK SHEET EXAMPLE

Day 7   The sum of the True Ranges for the first seven days equals 4.05; divided by 7 equals .58, times 3.00 equals 1.74. Since the market is in a down trend, we are looking for a point to go *Long*. Therefore, assuming a present *Short* trade, we add 1.74 to the lowest close of 51.10, giving a SAR of 52.84 which we put in the SAR column for Day 8.

Day 8   Using the ATR equation, we multiply the previous ATR by 6, add TR_1, which is .50 and obtain 3.98. We divide 3.98 by 7 and obtain the ATR of .57 times 3.00 which equals 1.71. Adding 1.71 to the lowest close of 51.10 gives 52.81 as the SAR for Day 9. We repeat this procedure until the price closes above the SAR, at which point we will take a *Long* position.

Day 16   The price closes above the SAR and we go *Long* on the close at 52.50. After the market closes, we calculate the ARC and subtract it from the highest close (the HI SIC) since entering the trade, which is the close today of 52.50. The SAR for Day 17 is 52.50 — 1.74 = 50.76.

Day 33   The price penetrated the SAR but closed above the SAR, so we are still *Long*. Notice how the SAR backs up to compensate for increased volatility after a new high has been made. Notice also that the SAR moves **in the direction** of the trade to compensate for decreased volatility.

Day 46   The price closed below the SAR and we reversed the position to *Short* on the close at 56.05. We compute the ARC and add it to 56.05 to obtain the SAR for Day 47 of 58.72.

On the following pages are charts showing this system in actual markets. This system does not make as many trades as the other systems in this book. The VOLATILITY SYSTEM is designed to pick up and hold on to the long-term moves.

It should be traded in those markets that are high on the COMMODITY SELECTION INDEX (Explained in Section IX).

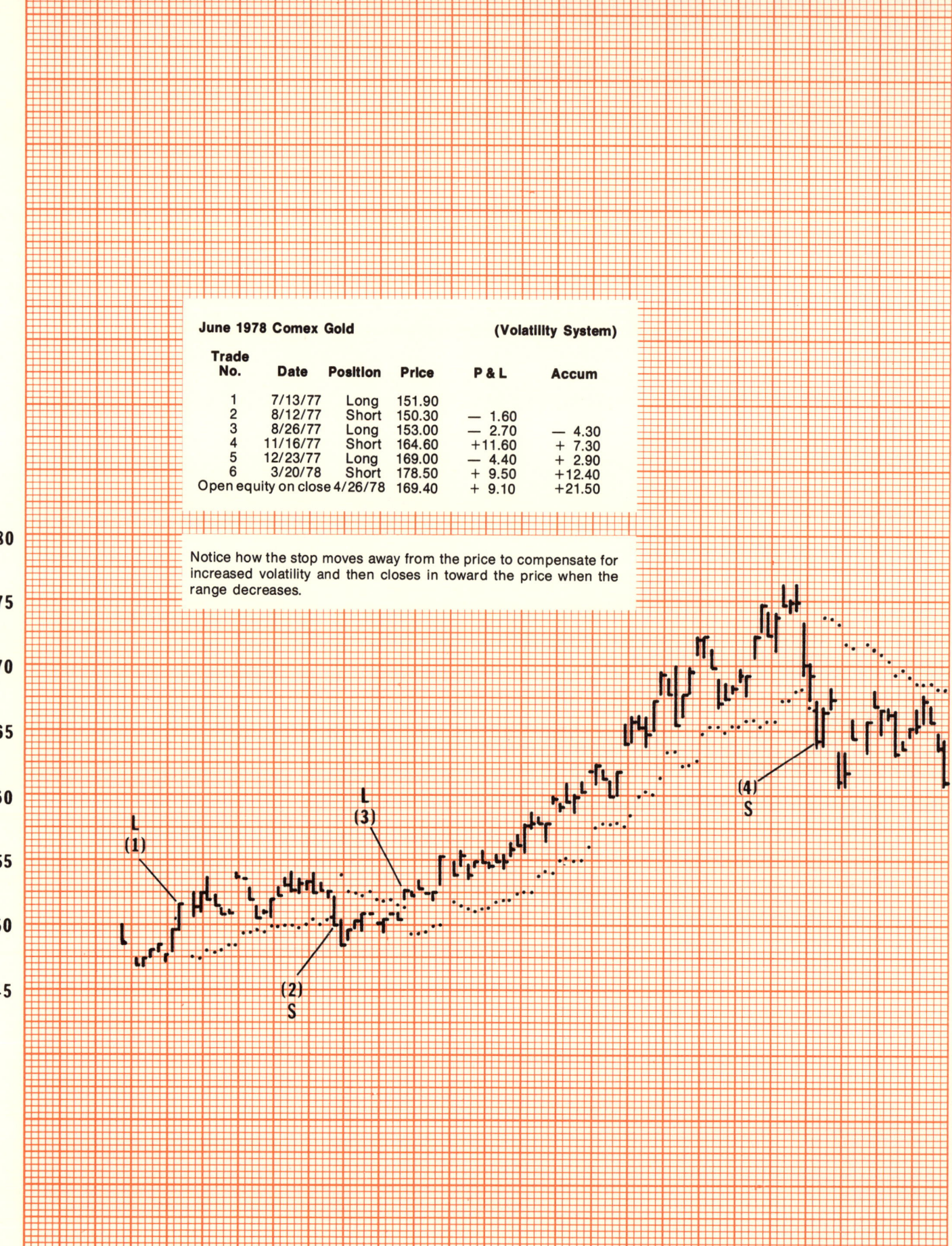

April 1978 Live Cattle **(Volatility System)**

Trade No.	Date	Position	Price	P & L	Accum
1	4/27/77	Short	44.82		
2	6/20/77	Long	42.05	+ 2.77	
3	7/12/77	Short	40.32	— 1.73	+ 1.04
4	9/ 8/77	Long	37.97	+ 2.35	+ 3.39
5	3/28/78	Out	53.67	+15.70	+19.09

Trade was exited on close on the last trading day for April Cattle.

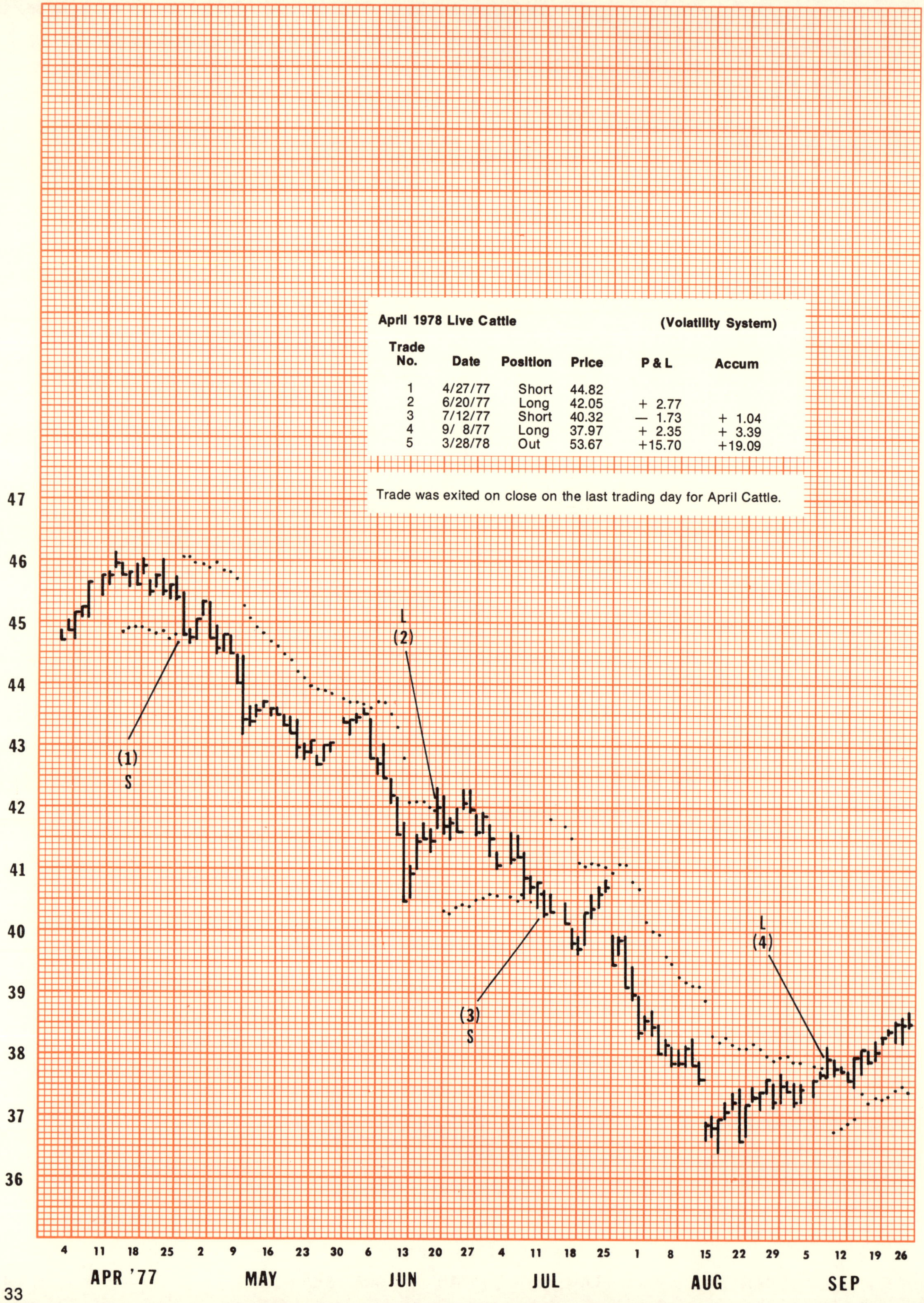

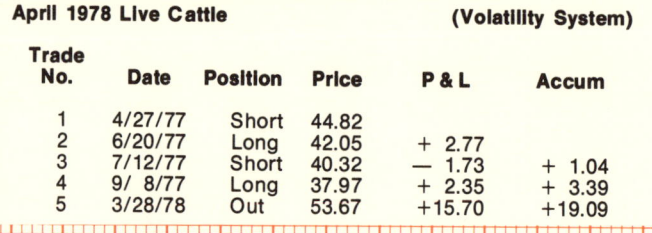

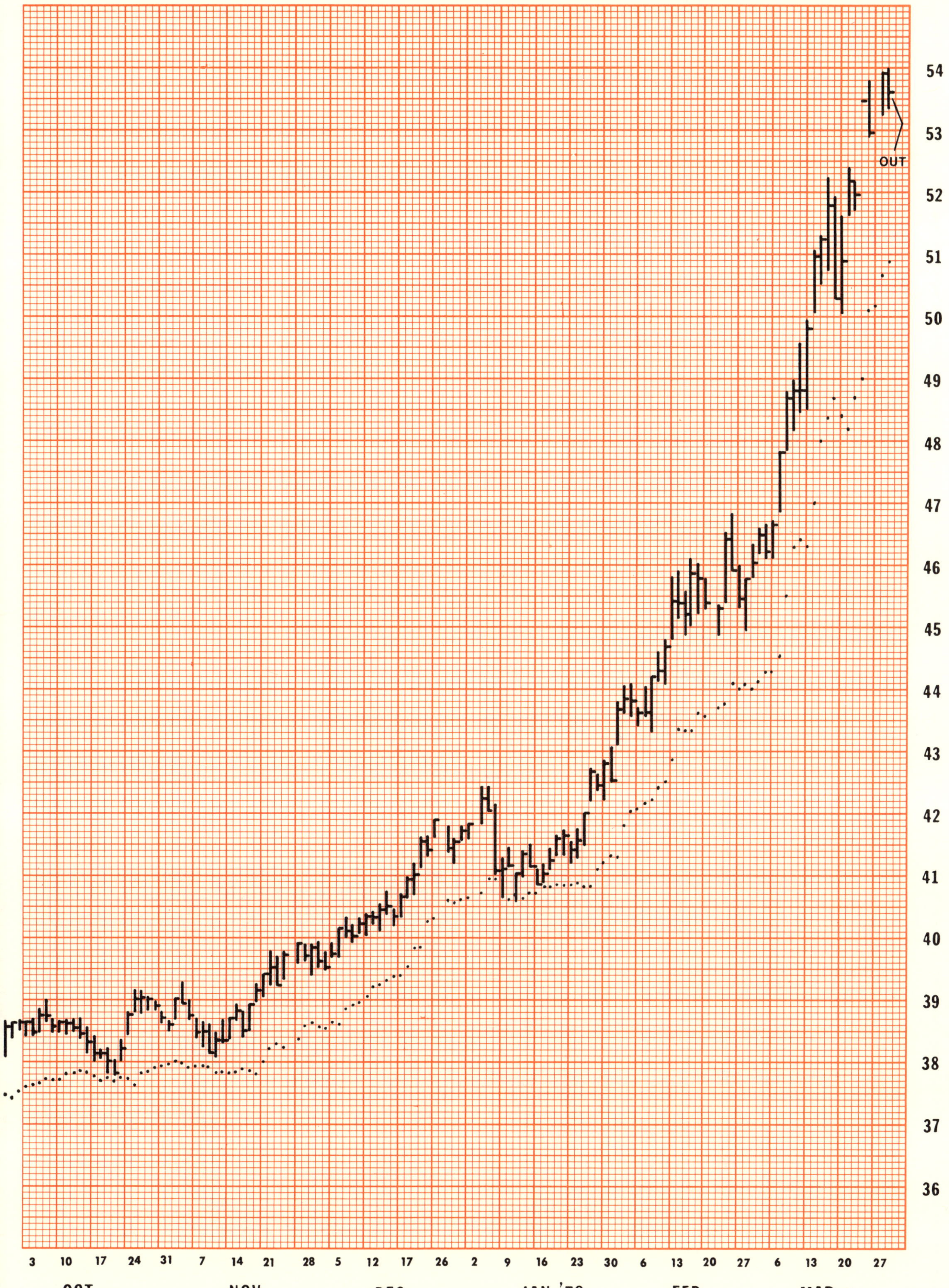
54
53
52
51
50
49
48
47
46
45
44
43
42
41
40
39
38
37
36
OUT
3
10
17
24
31
7
14
21
28
5
12
17
26
2
9
16
23
30
6
13
20
27
6
13
20
27
OCT
NOV
DEC
JAN '78
FEB
MAR

SECTION IV

DIRECTIONAL MOVEMENT

Directional movement is the most fascinating concept I have studied. Defining it is a little like chasing the end of a rainbow... you can see it, you know it's there, but the closer you get to it the more elusive it becomes. I have probably spent more time studying directional movement than any other concept. Certainly one of my most satisfying achievements was the day I was actually able to reduce this concept to an absolute mathematical equation.

Think of the implications of being able to rate the directional movement of any or all commodities or stocks on a scale of zero to one hundred. If you use a trend-following method, you would trade only those commodities that are in the upper end of the scale. If you are using a system that capitalizes on choppy or non-trending markets, then you would trade only those commodities at the lower end of the scale. Consider also, being able to define an **equilibrium point** where directional movement **up** is in equilibrium with directional movement **down**.

Much work has been done in defining technical trading **systems,** but very little work has been done in the area of defining **markets** relative to technical trading systems. Now let's look at how this *can* be done.

We will start with the smallest increment of directional movement. In Fig. 4.1, movement is obviously in the **up** direction. The magnitude of this **up** movement is the difference between points C and A. In effect, this is the high today minus the high yesterday. We will call this distance PLUS DM (+DM). Because the movement is **up** we consider only the highs.

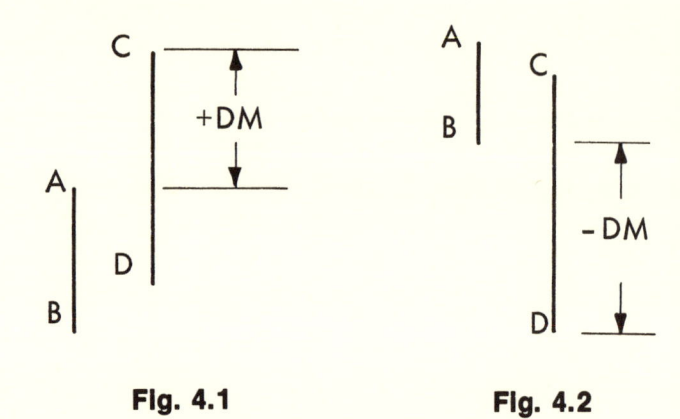

Fig. 4.1

Fig. 4.2

We disregard the distance between the lows; that is, points B and D.

In Fig. 4.2, the directional movement is obviously **down.** The directional distance is the difference between points B and D. This distance is considered to be a minus distance and is the difference between the low today and the low yesterday. Since the direction is obviously down, we are concerned only with the lows. We disregard the distance between the highs. We will call the difference between the lows, MINUS DM (—DM).

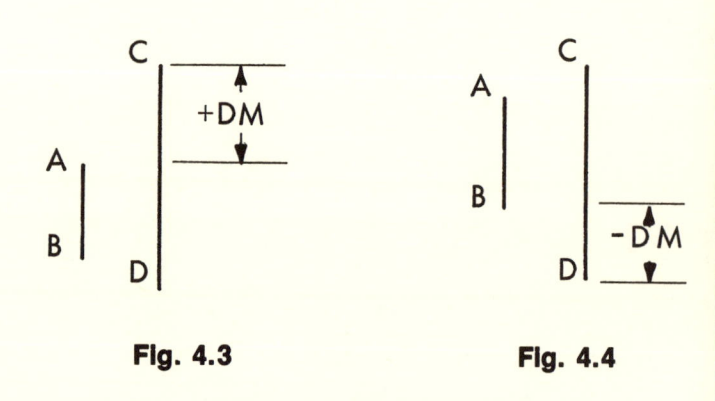

Fig. 4.3

Fig. 4.4

35

NEW CONCEPTS IN TECHNICAL TRADING SYSTEMS

Now, how do we handle an outside day? Look at Fig. 4.3. In this case, the directional movement is up because +DM is greater than —DM. **Directional movement must be either up or down — it cannot be a combination of both.** We therefore consider the **larger** DM for an **outside** day and disregard the smaller DM. Here, the DM is the distance between C and A and is **plus.**

In Fig. 4.4, only —DM is considered because it is larger than +DM.

Fig. 4.5

Fig. 4.6

How about an inside day? (Fig. 4.5) In this case, directional movement is zero. In Fig. 4.6, the directional movement is also zero.

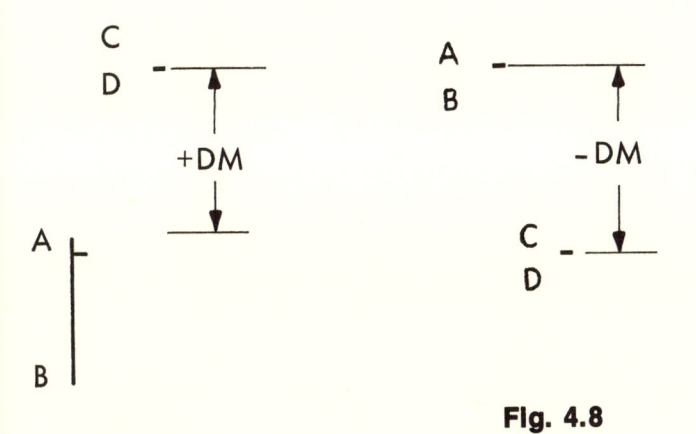

Fig. 4.7

Fig. 4.8

On a limit up day (Fig. 4.7), the +DM is C minus A. On a limit down day, (Fig. 4.8), the —DM is D minus B. These illustrations take into consideration every possible configuration that could occur between two days relative to directional movement. To sum the preceding in one sentence, we could say that the basic increment of directional movement is:

THE LARGEST PART OF TODAY'S RANGE THAT IS OUTSIDE YESTERDAY'S RANGE.

If the largest part of today's range is **above** yesterday's range, the DM is PLUS. If the largest part of today's range is **below** yesterday's range, the DM is MINUS.

To be meaningful, DM must be expressed as a function of range; that is, it must be relative to range. The range increment is today's TRUE RANGE (TR_1). This is the same true range we have used in previous chapters. It is the **largest** of the following:

(1) The distance between today's high and today's low.
(2) The distance between today's high and yesterday's close, or
(3) The distance between today's low and yesterday's close.

True range is always considered to be a positive number.

To make directional movement relative to range, we simply divide directional movement by the true range. This will give us what we will call the DIRECTIONAL INDICATOR (DI). The +DI and —DI equations below each express the DIRECTIONAL INDICATOR for **one day** which is indicated by the subscript $_1$.

$$+DI_1 = \frac{+DM_1}{TR_1}$$

$$-DI_1 = \frac{-DM_1}{TR_1}$$

If the day were an **up** day, the $+DI_1$ equation would be applicable; if the day were a **down** day, the $-DI_1$ equation would be applicable. We cannot have both directional movement **up** and directional movement **down** on the same day. Today is either UP or it is DOWN. In effect, the +DI is an expression of the percent of the true range that is UP for the day; the —DI is an expression of the percent of the true range that is DOWN for the day.

To make the DIRECTIONAL INDICATOR (DI) a useable tool, we must obtain the sum of the DIs for a period of time. We use 14 days because that is an average half-cycle period. This can be done by reviewing the preceding 14 days and determining the Directional Movement (DM_1) for each day. We also determine the True Range for each day. First, we add together all of the **True Ranges** for the 14 days. We will designate the sum of the 14 day's ranges as TR_{14}. Next, add together all of the Plus DM's ($+DM_1$) for the 14 days and call the sum $+DM_{14}$. Now go back and add all the Minus DM's ($-DM_1$) for the previous 14 days and call the sum $-DM_{14}$.

The equations for $+DI_{14}$ and $-DI_{14}$ are as follows:

$$+DI_{14} = \frac{+DM_{14}}{TR_{14}}$$

$$-DI_{14} = \frac{-DM_{14}}{TR_{14}}$$

(The definition "minus DM" is a description of downward movement. It is **not** treated as a minus number in the equation.)

Once we have determined the first $+DM_{14}$ and the first $-DM_{14}$, it is no longer necessary to keep up with 14 day's back data to determine the $+DM_{14}$ and $-DM_{14}$ for the following day. We use the previous day's data and an accumulation technique in this determination. The advantage to using the accumulation technique is:

(1) It eliminates the necessity of keeping up with 14 day's previous data.
(2) It incorporates a smoothing effect on the DM.

To obtain the new $+DM_{14}$ using the accumulation technique, take yesterday's $+DM_{14}$, divide it by 14 and subtract this amount from yesterday's $+DM_{14}$. Next, add back the $+DM_1$ for today, if any. The result is the $+DM_{14}$ for today.

$$\text{Today's } +DM_{14} = \text{Previous } +DM_{14} - \frac{\text{Previous } +DM_{14}}{14} + \text{Today's } +DM_1$$

We do the same thing with the $-DM_{14}$. We subtract 1/14th of yesterday's $-DM_{14}$ and add back the $-DM_1$ today, if any.

$$\text{Today's } -DM_{14} = \text{Previous } -DM_{14} - \frac{\text{Previous } -DM_{14}}{14} + \text{Today's } -DM_1$$

Each day we will be taking away 1/14th of the $+DM$ and 1/14th of the $-DM$. If the DM_1 (today) is minus, we will add its value back to the $-DM_{14}$. If the DM_1 (today) is plus, we will add it back to the $+DM_{14}$.

The same procedure is used on the TRUE RANGE. We reduce TR_{14} by 1/14th and add back to it the TRUE RANGE for today (TR_1). The result is our new TR_{14}.

$$\text{Today's TR}_{14} = \text{Previous TR}_{14} - \left[\frac{\text{Previous TR}_{14}}{14}\right] + \text{TR}_1$$

The $+DI_{14}$ is an indication of the percent of the total true range of the last 14 days which was **up**. The $-DI_{14}$ is an indication of the percent of the total true range of the last 14 days which was **down**. Both the $+DI_{14}$ and the $-DI_{14}$ are positive numbers.

If you are a little confused at this point, don't worry. We will stop here and go through an example step by step of everything discussed to this point. We will then show how to utilize the $+DI_{14}$ and the $-DI_{14}$ and then go on to the derivation of the DIRECTIONAL MOVEMENT INDEX which is the difference between $+DI_{14}$ and $-DI_{14}$ converted into a value that always falls between 0 and 100. First, though, let's look at an example on the following work sheet.

On the work sheet, we are following March '78 Chicago Wheat. Let's begin by looking at the first 14 days.

Columns #1 through #5 are self-explanatory.
Column #6 is the TRUE RANGE for the day.
Column #7 is the PLUS DM ($+DM_1$) for today.
Column #8 is the MINUS DM ($-DM_1$) for today.

Note on 6/7/77 that both the $+DM_1$ and the $-DM_1$ are zero. This is an inside day. Also, 6/16/77 is an inside day. For the first 14 days, we only fill in Columns #6, #7, and #8. At the end of 14 days, we obtain the **total** of Columns #6, #7 and #8.

At the end of 14 days, the total True Range, TR_{14} obtained from adding together each of the 14 day's true ranges (TR_1) is 41.00. The total $+DM_{14}$ obtained from adding together all of the numbers in Column #7 is 9.50. The total $-DM_{14}$ obtaining by summing the numbers in Column #8 is 14.00.

We are now, at Day 15, (6/21/77) ready to determine TR_{14} for today, $+DM_{14}$ for today and $-DM_{14}$ for today. The mathematics for obtaining TR_{14} for today are as follows:

$$\begin{aligned}
TR_{14}\text{ (today)} &= \text{Previous TR}_{14} - \left[\frac{\text{Previous TR}_{14}}{14}\right] + TR_1 \\
&= 41.00 - \left[\frac{41.00}{14}\right] + 5.25 \\
&= 41.00 - 2.93 + 5.25 = 43.32
\end{aligned}$$

The mathematics for obtaining $+DM_{14}$ are as follows: (in these equations, $+DM$ is written 'plus' and $-DM$ is written 'minus' so as not to be confused with $+$ and $-$ as mathematical operators).

$$\begin{aligned}
\text{Plus DM}_{14}\text{ (today)} &= \text{Previous Plus DM}_{14} - \left[\frac{\text{Previous Plus DM}_{14}}{14}\right] + \text{Plus DM}_1 \\
\text{Plus DM}_{14}\text{ (today)} &= 9.50 - \left[\frac{9.50}{14}\right] + 0 \\
\text{Plus DM}_{14}\text{ (today)} &= 9.50 - .68 + 0 = 8.82
\end{aligned}$$

The mathematics for determining $-DM_{14}$ are as follows:

$$\text{Minus DM}_{14}(\text{today}) = \text{Previous Minus DM}_{14} - \left[\frac{\text{Previous Minus DM}_{14}}{14}\right] + \text{Minus DM}_1$$

$$\text{Minus DM}_{14}(\text{today}) = 14.00 - \left[\frac{14.00}{14}\right] + 2.75$$

$$\text{Minus DM}_{14}(\text{today}) = 14.00 - 1.00 + 2.75 = 15.75$$

Note that in each case above, we decrease the previous total by 1/14th and then add back the applicable DM_1 for the day. For the TRUE RANGE Column, we always have a number to add back for the day; however, for the +DM there was nothing to add back because +DM on the 15th day was zero. For the —DM on the 15th day, we have 2.75 to add back.

In Column #9, insert TR_{14}, which is 43.32.
In Column #10, insert the $+DM_{14}$ which is 8.82.
In Column #11, insert the $-DM_{14}$ which is 15.75.

Now divide $+DM_{14}$ (in Column #10) by TR_{14} (in Column #9) as follows:

$$\frac{+DM_{14}}{TR_{14}} = \frac{8.82}{43.32} = .20 \times 100 = 20$$

We multiply the answer by 100 (or simply drop the decimal point) and put this number in Column #12. This number, 20, is the PLUS DIRECTIONAL INDICATOR (+DI). In effect, it implies that 20% of the True Range for the previous 14 days was **up**.

$$\frac{-DM_{14}}{TR_{14}} = \frac{15.75}{43.32} = .36 \times 100 = 36$$

Now we take our $-DM_{14}$ in Column #11 and divide it by the same TR_{14} in Column #9 and obtain .36. This is the MINUS DIRECTIONAL INDICATOR (—DI). Again, we either multiply by 100 or simply drop the decimal point and insert 36 in Column #13. In effect, this tells us that 36% of the True Range for the past 14 days was **down**.

Now let's analyze what we have here. If 20% of the True Range for the past 14 days was up and 36% of the True Range for the past 14 days was down, then we add these two figures together and determine that 56% of the True Range was directional — either up or down; therefore, 44% of the True Range was non-directional.

Here is the real breakthrough — TRUE DIRECTIONAL MOVEMENT is the DIFFERENCE BETWEEN $+DI_{14}$ and $-DI_{14}$. This is the important concept. **The more directional the movement of a commodity or stock, the greater will be the difference between** $+DI_{14}$ and $-DI_{14}$. Each day that we have a plus directional movement, we are **adding** to $+DI_{14}$. At the same time, we are **subtracting** from $-DI_{14}$. If the direction were up for 14 or more consecutive days, the $+DI_{14}$ would have a large value and the $-DI_{14}$ would approach zero. Therefore, the difference between the two would be very large.

Conversely, if the price were to go down for 14 or more consecutive days, giving us a —DM for every day, we are **adding** to the —DI$_{14}$ and **subtracting** from the +DI$_{14}$, thereby increasing the difference between +DI$_{14}$ and —DI$_{14}$.

If the price were meandering in a sideways direction, then the difference between +DI$_{14}$ and —DI$_{14}$ would be very small. This tells us the price is moving **non-directionally**. Notice also that we can have a high directional movement value in a very slow moving market because directional movement is a function of daily range. Conversely we can have a low directional movement value in a very volatile market.

Now let's go back to our work sheet. We take the **difference** between +DI$_{14}$ and —DI$_{14}$ (i.e., the difference of the numbers in Column #12 and #13) and put this value in Column #14.

Column #14 is the DI DIFFERENCE.

In this case, the DI DIFFERENCE is 16.

We stated previously that the **sum** of the plus directional movement and the minus directional movement (+DI$_{14}$ added to —DI$_{14}$) represents the total amount of the past 14 day's ranges that moved directionally . . . either plus or minus. We put this number in Column #15.

Column #15 is the **sum** of Columns #12 and #13.

In this case, 20 + 36 = 56.

We are now ready to fill in Column #16, which is our DIRECTIONAL MOVEMENT INDEX (DX). This is obtained by dividing the **difference** between +DI$_{14}$ and —DI$_{14}$ by the **sum** of +DI$_{14}$ and —DI$_{14}$.

We divide 16 by 56 and either multiply by 100 or drop the decimal point and we have 29, the DX for today.

This equation results in a DX that must always be **between 0 and 100**. The higher the DX, the more directional the movement; the lower the DX, the less directional the movement. Notice that whether the price movement is up or down, **it makes no difference relative to the value of the DX.**

Suppose that the price goes straight up for 14 days or more and then turns around and goes straight down for 14 days or more. The DX will decrease as the price tops out and starts down, and it will increase again as the price continues down. Both the **up move** and the **down move** represent good directional movement. As the price tops out and starts down, the **difference** between the +DI$_{14}$ and —DI$_{14}$ **will decrease**, go to zero and then increase. That is, as the price is going up, +DI$_{14}$ will be a large number and —DI$_{14}$ will be a small number. As the price tops out and goes down, **the equilibrium point will be reached,** then the —DI$_{14}$ will increase and the +DI$_{14}$ will decrease and therefore the **difference** will again increase.

In order to smooth out this action relative to DX, and make DX indicative of both extreme **up** and **down** price movement, the period for determining DX must be twice the period for determining +DI$_{14}$ and —DI$_{14}$. This can be accomplished simply by using a 14 day average of DX. We compute the DX for 14 days and then at that time begin determining the AVERAGE DIRECTIONAL MOVEMENT INDEX (ADX) from the previous day's ADX.

At this point you have probably already figured out that you go *Long* when +DI$_{14}$ crosses over —DI$_{14}$ and you go *Short* when —DI$_{14}$ crosses over +DI$_{14}$ and that you only trade the top five or six commodities that are highest on the **ADX Scale**. If so, you have a good understanding of the text so far, but there is a little more to it than that. Before we take up the last part of this concept, let's review the above discussion by picking up at Day 16 (6/22/77) on the work sheet.

DAILY WORK SHEET

DIRECTIONAL MOVEMENT INDEX

	(1) DATE	(2) OPEN	(3) HIGH	(4) LOW	(5) CLOSE	(6) TR 1	(7) +DM 1	(8) −DM 1	(9) TR 14	(10) +DM 14	(11) −DM 14	(10)÷(9) (12) +DI 14	(11)÷(9) (13) −DI 14	(12)− (14) DI D
1	6-1-77		274	272	272.75									
2	2		273.25	270.25	270.75	3.00	0	1.75						
3	3		272	269.75	270	2.25	0	.50						
4	6M		270.75	268	269.25	2.75	0	1.75						
5	7		270	269	269.75	1.00	0	0						
6	8		270.50	268	270	2.50	0	1.00						
7	9		268.50	266.50	266.50	3.50	0	1.50						
8	10		265.50	263	263.25	3.50	0	3.50						
9	13M		262.50	259	260.25	4.25	0	4.00						
10	14		263.50	260	263	3.50	1.00	0						
11	15		269.50	263	266.50	6.50	6.00	0						
12	16		267.25	265	267	2.25	0	0						
13	17		267.50	265.50	265.75	2.00	.25	0						
14	20M		269.75	266	268.50	4.00	2.25	0						
	TOTALS					41.00	9.50	14.00						
15	21		268.25	263.25	264.25	5.25	0	2.75	43.32	8.82	15.75	20	36	16
16	22		264	261.50	264	2.75	0	1.75	42.98	8.19	16.37	19	38	19
17	23		268	266.25	266.50	4.00	4.00	0	43.91	11.60	15.20	26	35	9
18	24		266	264.25	265.25	2.25	0	2.00	43.02	10.77	16.11	25	37	12
19	27M		274	267	273	8.75	8.00	0	48.70	18.00	14.96	37	31	6
20	28		277.50	273.50	276.75	4.50	3.50	0	49.72	20.21	13.89	41	28	13
21	29		277	272.50	273	4.50	0	1.00	50.67	18.77	13.90	37	27	10
22	30		272	269.50	270.25	3.50	0	3.00	50.55	17.43	15.91	34	31	4
23	7-1-77		267.75	264	266.75	6.25	0	5.50	53.19	16.18	20.27	30	38	8
24	5T		269.25	263	263	6.25	1.50	0	55.64	16.52	18.82	30	34	4
25	6		266	263.50	265.50	3.00	0	0	54.67	15.34	17.48	28	32	4
26	7		265	262	262.25	3.50	0	1.50	54.26	14.24	17.73	26	33	7
27	8		264.75	261.50	262.75	3.25	0	.50	53.63	13.22	16.96	25	32	7
28	11M		261	255.50	255.50	7.25	0	6.00	57.05	12.28	21.75	22	38	16
	TOTAL													
29	12		257.50	253	253	4.50	0	2.50	57.47	11.40	22.70	20	39	19
30	13		259	254	257.50	6.00	1.50	0	59.36	12.09	21.08	20	36	16
31	14		259.75	257.50	257.50	2.25	.75	0	57.37	11.98	19.57	21	34	13
32	15		257.25	250	250	7.50	0	7.50	60.77	11.12	25.67	18	42	24
33	18m		250	247	249.15	3.00	0	3.00	59.43	10.33	26.84	17	45	28
34	19		254.25	252.75	253.75	4.50	4.25	0	59.68	13.84	24.92	23	42	19
35	20		254	250.50	251.25	3.50	0	2.25	58.92	12.85	25.39	22	43	21
36	21		253.25	250.25	250.50	3.00	0	.25	57.71	11.93	23.83	21	41	20
37	22		253.25	251	253	2.75	0	0	56.34	11.08	22.13	20	39	19
38	25m		251.75	250.50	251.50	2.50	0	.50	54.82	10.29	21.05	19	38	19
39	26		253	249.50	250	3.50	1.25	0	54.40	10.80	19.55	20	36	16
40	27		251.50	245.25	245.75	6.25	0	4.25	56.16	10.05	22.40	18	39	21
41	28		246.25	240	242.75	6.25	0	5.25	58.96	9.31	26.05	16	44	28
42	29		244.25	241.25	243.50	3.00	0	0	57.15	8.64	24.19	15	42	27

COMMODITY Chicago Wheat   CONTRACT MONTH March 1978

K _____

(15) DI SUM	(16) DX	(17) ADX	ACTION and ORDER	ADXR	ATR 14	CSI
56	29					
57	33					
61	15					
62	19					
68	9					
69	19					
64	16					
66	6					
68	12					
64	6					
60	7					
59	12					
57	12					
60	21					
	222	16				
59	32	17				
56	29	18				
55	24	18				
60	40	20				
62	45	22				
65	29	22				
65	32	23				
62	32	23				
59	32	24				
57	33	25				
56	28	25				
57	37	26				
60	47	27			22	4.21
57	47	29			23	4.13

42

DIRECTIONAL MOVEMENT — WORK SHEET EXPLANATION

Day 16: We put in the high, low and close and then determine the **True Range** to be 2.75. The +DM is 0 and the —DM is 1.75. To determine TR_{14} for Column #9, we make the following calculation:

$$TR_{14} = 43.32 - \left[\frac{43.32}{14}\right] + 2.75$$

$$= 43.32 - 3.09 + 2.75$$

$$= 42.98$$

To determine the $+DM_{14}$ for Column #10, we make the following calculation:

$$+DM_{14} = 8.82 - \left[\frac{8.82}{14}\right] + 0$$

$$= 8.82 - .63 + 0$$

$$= 8.19$$

To determine the $-DM_{14}$ for Column #11, we make the following calculation:

$$-DM_{14} = 15.75 - \left[\frac{15.75}{14}\right] + 1.75$$

$$= 15.75 - 1.13 + 1.75$$

$$= 16.37$$

Now divide Column #10 by Column #9, drop the decimal point and obtain 19 for $+DI_{14}$ which goes in Column #12:

$$\text{Column \#12:} \quad \frac{8.19}{42.98} = .19 \times 100 = 19$$

Now divide Column #11 by Column #9, drop the decimal and obtain 38 for $-DI_{14}$ which goes in Column #13

$$\text{Column \#13:} \quad \frac{16.37}{42.98} = .38 \times 100 = 38$$

Now take the **difference** between Column #12 and Column #13 and put the DI DIFFERENCE in Column #14.

Column #14: 38 — 19 = 19

Now take the **sum** of Column #12 and Column #13 and put the result in Column #15.

Column #15: 39 + 19 = 57

Now divide Column #14 by Column #15, drop the decimal and put the result in Column #16.

Column #16: $\dfrac{19}{57} = 33$ **This is the DX.**

Follow this procedure for the next 14 days and you will have the routine firmly in mind. On the 28th day, 7/11/77, we have enough previous information to calculate the first AVERAGE DIRECTIONAL MOVEMENT INDEX (ADX).

We obtain the ADX on Day 28 by adding together the 14 previous numbers in Column #16 and dividing this total by 14. The result, 16, is the ADX for Day 28 (7/11/77). To obtain the ADX for the 29th day, 7/12/77, we use the moving average equation because now we are dealing with averages instead of totals. We multiply yesterday's ADX by 13, add today's DX and divide the total by 14. The procedure is as follows:

$$\text{Today's ADX} = \frac{\text{Previous ADX times 13 Plus DX today}}{14}$$

$$= \frac{(16 \times 13) + 32}{14}$$

$$= \frac{208 + 32}{14}$$

$$= 17.14 \text{ (which rounds off to 17)}$$

We put the result of this calculation, 17, in Column #17. The calculations are relatively simple and will become second nature very quickly to those who follow this method. The nice thing about this method is that once you obtain your first ADX you no longer have to look at previous data beyond yesterday. It takes only a minute or two a day to write down the information and run through the calculations on a small electronic calculator. You'll be surprised at how easy it is to follow once you have done it for a week or so.

This is all the information we need to follow the Directional Movement Index. However, there are three columns left on the work sheet which are:

ADXR — AVERAGE DIRECTIONAL MOVEMENT INDEX RATING

ATR_{14} — AVERAGE 14 DAY TRUE RANGE

CSI — COMMODITY SELECTION INDEX

These three entities pertain to the COMMODITY SELECTION INDEX (CSI) which is explained in Section IX. These columns have been added to the work sheet because this work sheet contains most of the information used to calculate the CSI.

At this point we will discuss the ADXR and the ATR_{14}. The ADXR is the final number which is used to rate all of the commodities, currencies, stocks, etc., on a rating scale which is indicative of directional movement. The ADXR is simply the ADX today plus the ADX 14 days ago divided by 2.

$$\text{ADXR} = \frac{\text{ADX}_{\text{Today}} + \text{ADX}_{\text{14 Days Ago}}}{2}$$

Since the ADXR is used only as a rating of directional movement, it must be indicative of directional movement but at the same time must have a minimum fluctuation when directional movement changes direction.

The ADX, when plotted, tends to form a sine curve on the ADX scale.

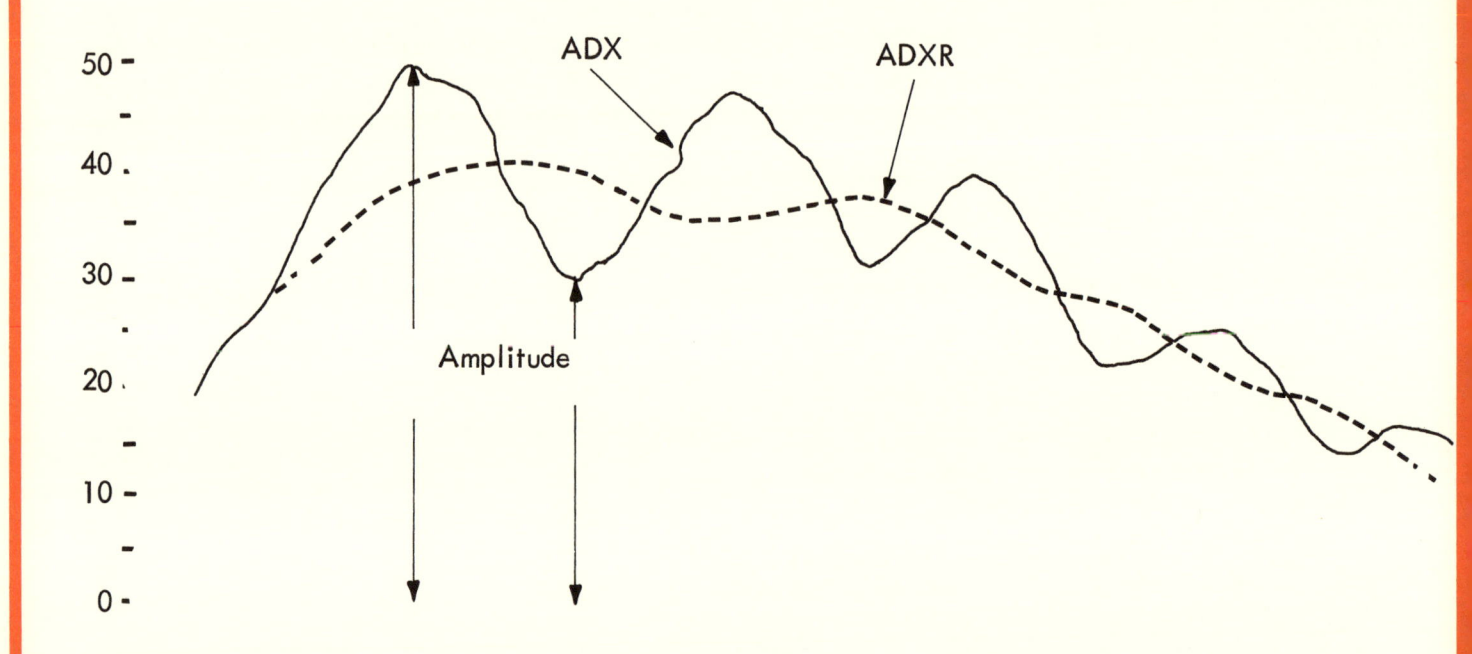

Fig. 4.10

The amplitude of the curve is measured from the zero line. The peaks and valleys of the ADX curve indicate a change of direction. If the major trend is down, the peaks would be low price points and the valleys would be high price points. If the major trend is up, the peaks would be high price points and the valleys would be low price points.

The higher the amplitude, the higher is the directional movement in one direction, either up or down, which is indicative of the major trend. The greater the distance between the peaks and valleys, the greater are the reactions to the trend. If the reactions are of significant duration and distance, the trend-following system will be profitable in both directions.

The ADXR must be indicative of good directional movement, but it must not overly fluctuate at equilibrium points. This is achieved by taking the average of a 14 day differential of the ADX.

The directional movement concept is not the easiest concept to grasp quickly.

Good directional movement is not simply straight up or straight down movement. It is also good up and down movement in **excess of the equilibrium point. This, in effect, is what the ADX measures.** The equilibrium point is reached when $+DI_{14}$ equals $-DI_{14}$.

In Fig. 4.11, the ADX will have a low value. The swings in the following illustration represent PRICE SWINGS.

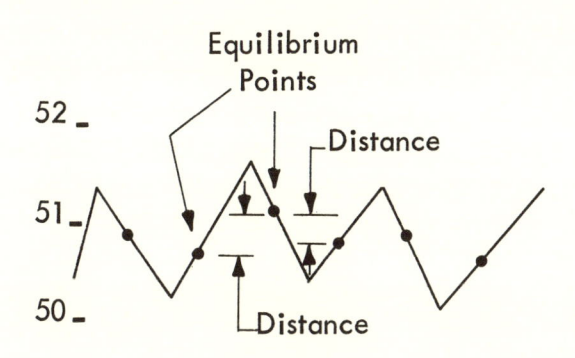

Fig. 4.11

The distance between the equilibrium points is relatively small.

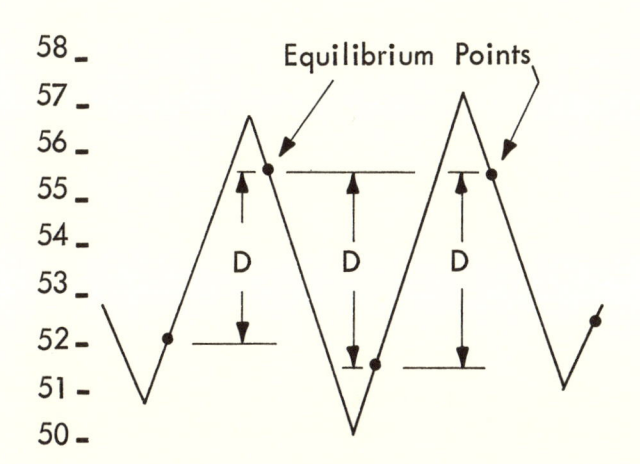

Fig. 4.12

In Fig. 4.12, the ADX will be higher because the distance between the equilibrium points is larger.

In Fig. 4.13, the ADX will have a higher value yet, because the equilibrium point was only reached one time, which was the turn down.

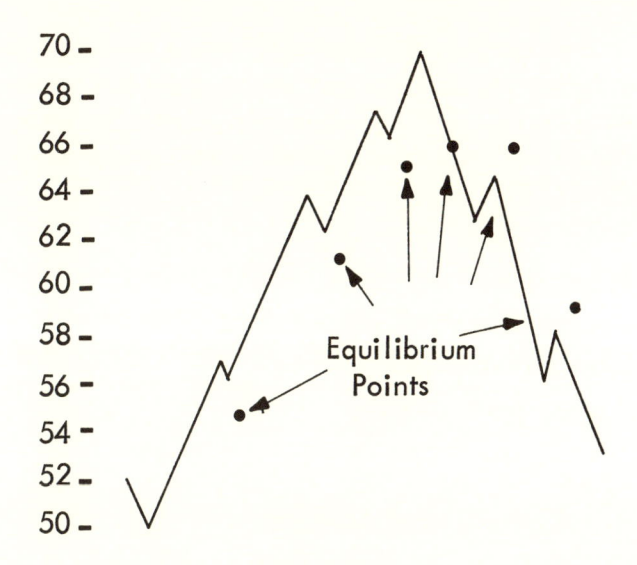

Fig. 4.13

Now let's look at the other extreme:

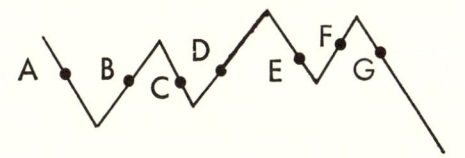

Fig. 4.14

The distance between equilibrium point B and C is 0. If we had bought at B and sold at C, we would have broken even. Suppose we had sold at E and bought at F. We would have had a loss. There is some directional movement because there is some distance between E and F.

This is indicative of market action when the ADXR is less than 20. When the ADXR is above 25, then the equilibrium points widen out. When directional movement is high relative to a 14 day period, then the equilibrium points come immediately after the turn rather than halfway up the next swing as happened at points B, D and F.

Much can be learned from an intensive study of this concept and the interactions of the lines made by $+DI_{14}$ and $-DI_{14}$ and ADX when charted. We will touch on some of the more obvious ones after we discuss the Directional Movement System.

On the work sheet, the first ADXR number of 22 on Day 41 was obtained by adding the ADX of 27 to the ADX 14 days ago, which was 16, and dividing the sum by 2:

ADXR = 27 + 16 = 43 ÷ 2 = 21.5
(round off to 22)

ATR_{14} is simply the Average TR_{14} which is obtained by dividing TR_{14} by 14.

ATR_{14} = 58.96 ÷ 14 = 4.21

The CSI and the constant K are explained in Section IX.

DIRECTIONAL MOVEMENT SYSTEM

The system itself is extremely simple. When $+DI_{14}$ crosses above $-DI_{14}$, a *Long* position is taken. The position is reversed when $-DI_{14}$ crosses above $+DI_{14}$. For best results, the system should be traded on markets which are **high** on the CSI scale.

As a rule of thumb, the system will be profitable on commodities that have an ADXR value above 25. When the ADXR drops below 20, then do not use a trend-following system. There are two systems in the book that can be used in a market with an ADXR less than 20 to 25. They are the **Trend Balance Point System** and the **Reaction Trend System.**

There is one more rule to following the Directional Movement System, and that is, the **Extreme Point Rule.**

On the day that $+DI_{14}$ and $-DI_{14}$ cross, use the extreme price made that day as the reverse point.

If you are *Long* the reverse point is the **low** made on the day of crossing. If you are *Short*, the reverse point is the **high** made on the day of crossing. Stay with this point, if not stopped out, even if the indexes stay crossed contrary to your position for several days.

I have noticed that the equilibrium point made by the Directional Movement System seems to be a critical point regardless of whether or not a market is going to turn around. Often the extreme price point made on the day that the indexes cross will not be penetrated again and the market will turn back in the direction of the open position.

The entry and reverse rules are so simple that it is not necessary to go through a work sheet example. Instead, we will discuss some significant interaction between lines made by $+DI_{14}$ and $-DI_{14}$ and the ADX when plotted on a bar chart.

For an example, we have used the bar chart of March 1978 Wheat. In July and August, the trend is down. The $-DI_{14}$ line is above the $+DI_{14}$ line and the DI Difference is relatively large. The ADX line is increasing. When the ADX line goes above the $-DI_{14}$ line, a turning point is indicated. The reason is that $-DI_{14}$ is beginning to wane but the ADX is still increasing because $+DI_{14}$ is still decreasing; therefore, the DI Difference is still large. The turning point often occurs concurrent with the first down turn of the ADX line **after** the ADX has crossed **above both** the DI_{14} lines.

On this chart, notice that the ADX line turned down (after crossing **above both** DI lines) two days after the bottom. The next ADX turn down (after crossing **above both** DI lines) was three days after the first intermediate top made on October 4, 1977. The next turn down (again, after crossing **above both** DI lines) was one day after the top made on November 21, 1977.

Notice that this indicator can only occur at favorable points **in the direction** of the major trend. When this occurs, it is seldom a bad time to take some profits. If you want to stay with the major trend, you will usually get a better buy point than the point at which you took profits. There is nothing wrong with exiting the system trade when this occurs and reentering in the direction of the next crossing of the DI lines or reentering if the ADX line again turns up.

Sometimes in a rip-roaring bull market approaching a blow-off stage, the ADX will turn up again after turning down while above both DI lines. In this situation, you may want to wait for the crossing; however, if you are trading several contracts, it is still a good time to pocket some profit at the first down turn of the ADX if it is above both DI lines.

Another interesting thing is that when the ADX line goes **below both** of the DI lines, then it is time to stop trading . . . at least, stop trading a trend-following system.

Now let's look at some examples of the Extreme Point Rule. On October 13, the $+DI_{14}$ line crossed below the $-DI_{14}$ line, giving a signal to reverse our *Long* position. We put our stop at the low of the day at 251.50, but this stop was never touched. On October 21, $+DI_{14}$ equaled $-DI_{14}$ but did not cross, so no action was indicated.

Again, on January 23, the $+DI_{14}$ line crossed above the $-DI_{14}$ line; however, we maintained the *Short* position because the high point made on January 23 was never penetrated.

Study the other chart in light of the discussion of the Wheat chart. Notice how this system follows the big moves and at times takes significant reactions without reversing. Notice also how quickly the position is reversed back in the direction of the major trend if the major trend continues.

I know that for many, the Directional Movement concept and its implications have not been easy to comprehend; however, those who pursue it will be rewarded for their effort. Here is a system that gives you a definitive entry and exit point in the market and at the same time tells you whether or not you should be trading that particular market.

Another way that the $+DI_{14}$ and $-DI_{14}$ indicators can be used is as a backup on whatever system you may prefer to use and also as an early indicator of bottoms and tops when the ADX line goes above both DI lines and then turns down. Suppose, for instance, as a long-term trader you have been watching a commodity go down for several months and are looking for a buy point. This system usually gives an early indication of the bottom by a turn down of the ADX and a confirmation when $+DI$ goes above $-DI_{14}$

Another alternative is to use the ADX as a trend indicator for the other systems in this book . . . or any system you wish to use. When $+DI_{14}$ crosses above $-DI_{14}$, take only the *Long* trades; when $-DI_{14}$ crosses above $+DI_{14}$ take only the *Short* trades.

I'm not going to rate the systems in this book because one trader's cup of tea may be another's nemesis. However, suffice it to say, for the serious trader who is interested in making profits, this chapter alone is worth many times the cost of this book.

Since this section is closely related to the Commodity Selection Index, it may be a good idea to skip to Section IX when finished with this section.

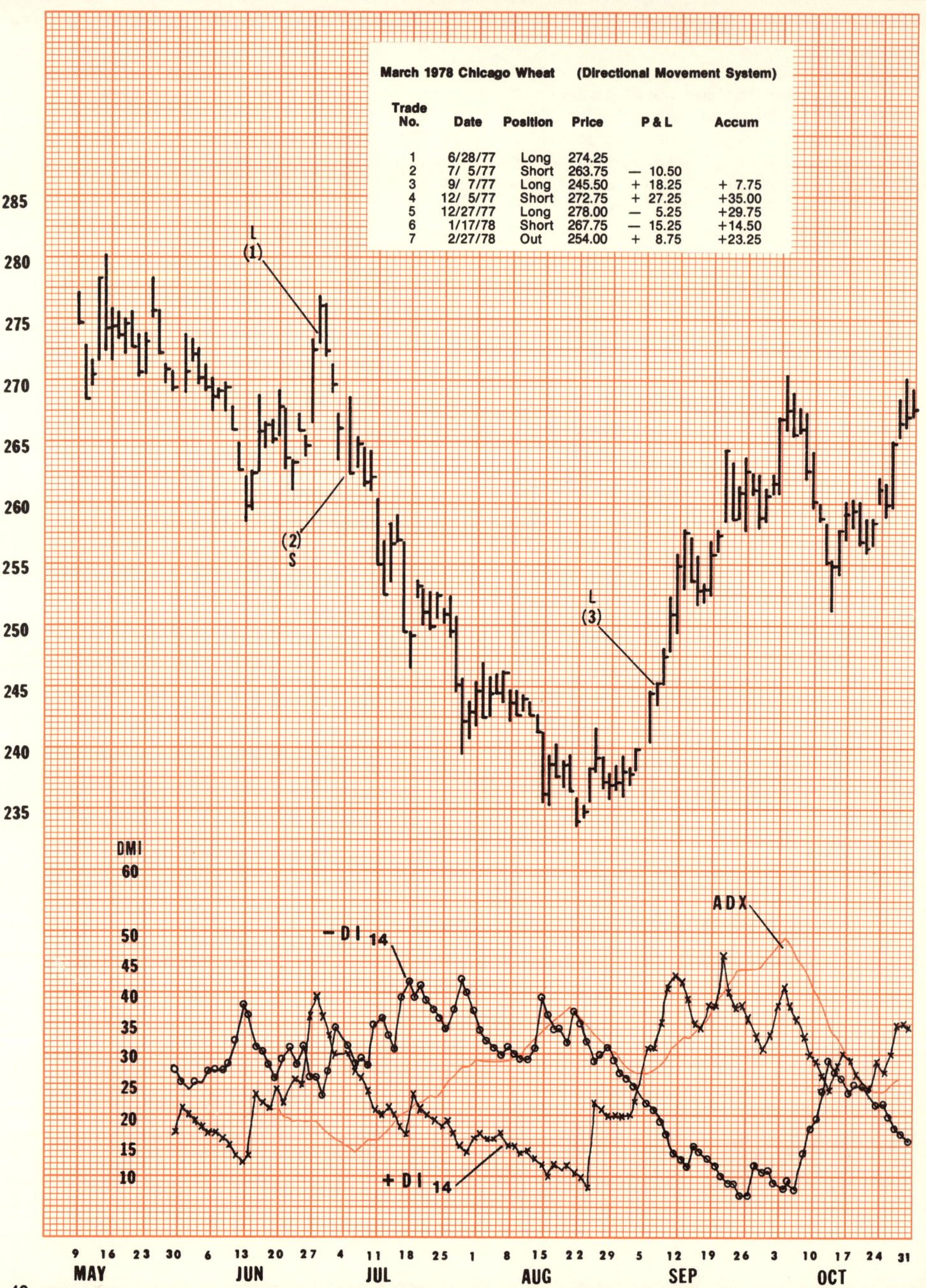

March 1978 Chicago Wheat (Directional Movement System)

Trade No.	Date	Position	Price	P & L	Accum
1	6/28/77	Long	274.25		
2	7/ 5/77	Short	263.75	− 10.50	+ 7.75
3	9/ 7/77	Long	245.50	+ 18.25	+35.00
4	12/ 5/77	Short	272.75	+ 27.25	+35.00
5	12/27/77	Long	278.00	− 5.25	+29.75
6	1/17/78	Short	267.75	− 15.25	+14.50
7	2/27/78	Out	254.00	+ 8.75	+23.25

49

295
290
285
280
275
270
265
260
255
250
L
(5)
(4)
S
(6)
S
(7)
OUT
DMI
60
50
45
40
35
30
25
20
15
10
7
14
21
28
5
12
19
26
2
9
16
23
30
6
13
20
27
NOV
DEC
JAN
FEB

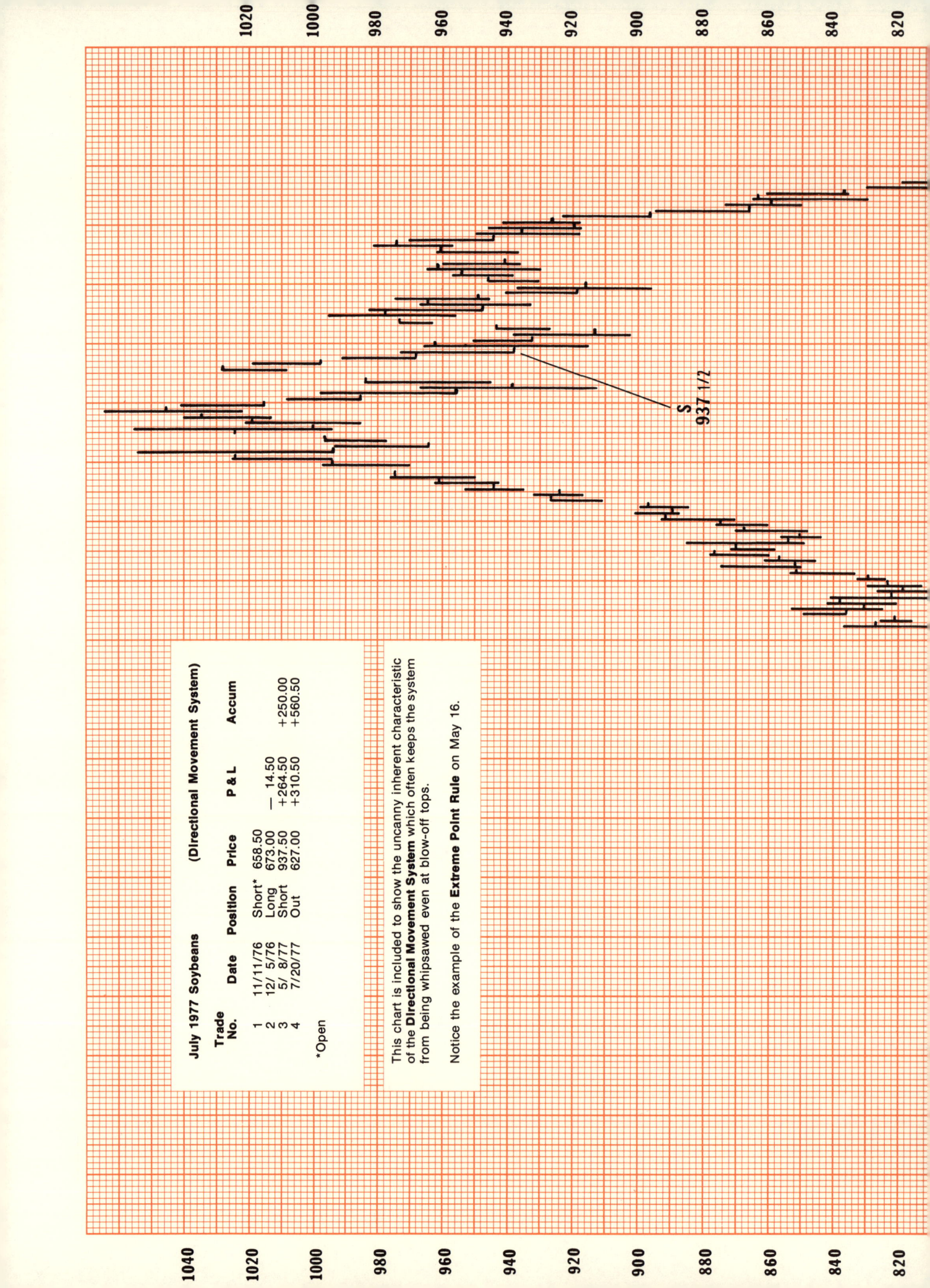

July 1977 Soybeans (Directional Movement System)

Trade No.	Date	Position	Price	P & L	Accum
1	11/11/76	Short*	658.50		
2	12/ 5/76	Long	673.00	− 14.50	
3	5/ 8/77	Short	937.50	+264.50	+250.00
4	7/20/77	Out	627.00	+310.50	+560.50

*Open

This chart is included to show the uncanny inherent characteristic of the **Directional Movement System** which often keeps the system from being whipsawed even at blow-off tops.

Notice the example of the **Extreme Point Rule** on May 16.

S 937 1/2

800
780
760
740
720
700
680
660
640
620
600
580
70
65
60
55
50
45
40
35
30
25
20
15
10
673
S
on
open
658 1/2
ADX
+DI14
−DI14
626
out
on
close
18 25 1 8 15 22 29 6 13 20 27 3 10 17 24 31 7 14 21 28 7 14 21 28 4 11 18 25 2 9 16 23 30 6 13 20 29 4 11 18
OCT '76
NOV
DEC
JAN '77
FEB
MAR
APR
MAY
JUN
JUL

SECTION V

THE MOMENTUM CONCEPT

One of the most useful concepts in technical trading is that of momentum; yet, for many traders, momentum is also one of the hardest concepts to understand. Momentum can be thought of as acceleration and deceleration.

In this discussion, upward momentum (acceleration) will be considered as 'plus' and downward momentum (deceleration) will be considered as 'minus'. Let's look at an example illustrating momentum.

Suppose that Pork Bellies closes one cent above the previous close for five consecutive days. The acceleration is zero. Conversely, if Bellies closes down one cent from the previous close for five consecutive days, the deceleration would also be zero. Now let's go back to the case where Bellies closes up one cent from the previous close for five consecutive days.

For the momentum factor to be **above** zero, it would be necessary for the price to close up **more** than one cent, so let's say that on the sixth day, the price closed up one and a half cents from the previous close. Now we have a plus momentum factor which is acceleration for the sixth day. On the seventh day, for the momentum to stay positive, the price must close up **more** than one and a half cents from the previous close. If the close on the seventh day were exactly one and a half cents more than the previous close, the momentum factor would again be zero. Now suppose that on the following day, Bellies closed up only one and a quarter cents more than the previous close. We would now have deceleration, or a minus momentum factor.

In Fig. 5.1, each point on the curve represents the closing price of a stock or commodity. Notice that from Days 1 through 9, each close is not only higher than the previous close, it is higher than the previous close by an **ever in-**

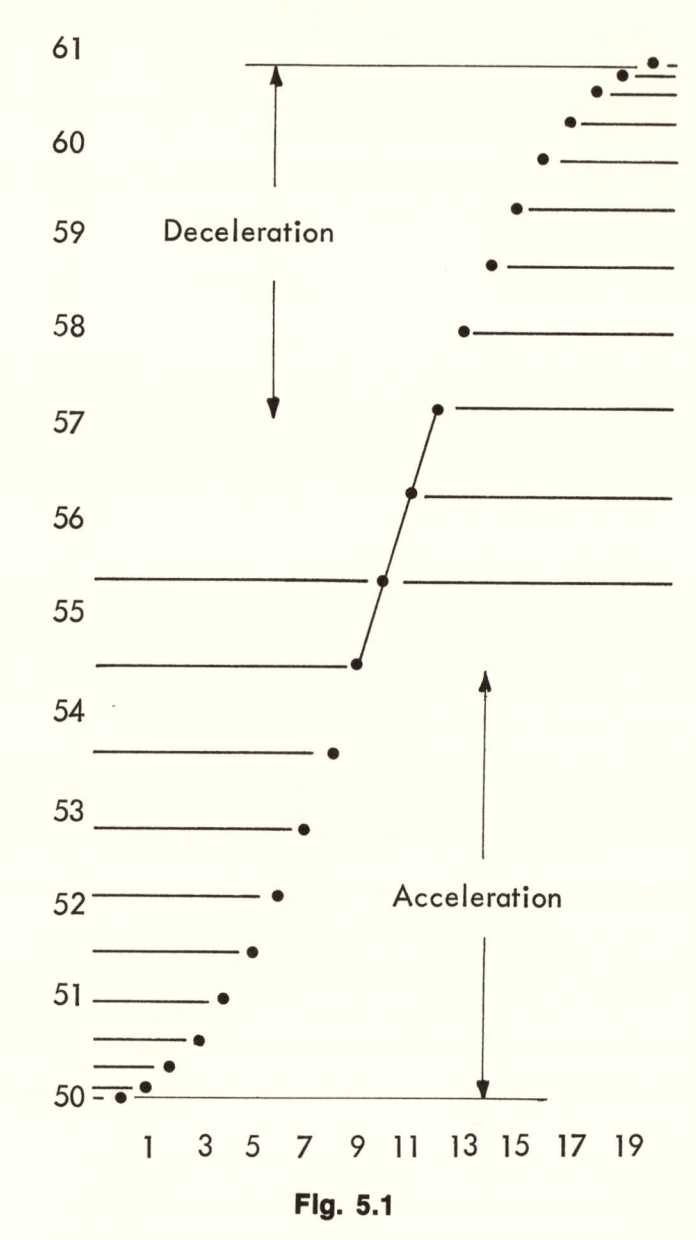

Fig. 5.1

creasing amount. Therefore, the price from Day 1 through 9 is accelerating and has a plus momentum factor. On Days 10 through 12, there is no acceleration or deceleration because the curve becomes a straight line. The price closed up exactly the same amount for each of these days, making a zero momentum factor for Days 9 through 12.

On Days 13 through 20, the price is closing up from the previous close; however, each close is a smaller distance up from the previous close and the price is beginning to decelerate and the momentum factors are minus.

THE TREND BALANCE POINT SYSTEM

The momentum system set forth here utilizes this concept in a most unique way. This system will satisfy traders and brokers who like a lot of action. It will usually make three to five trades a week. It takes small consistent profits and therefore the percentage of correct trades will be quite high compared to most technical systems.

In this system we use only close prices to compute the momentum factor. The system is not a true reversal system because profits are taken at a target. The indicator that tells whether the trade should be *Long* or *Short* in the market is the MOMENTUM FACTOR.

Now let's see how this momentum factor is calculated. **The momentum factor is the difference between the close price today and the close price two days ago.** It is important to note that we always take today's close first and subtract **from it** the close two days ago. This means that the difference may then be either 'plus' or 'minus'.

Day	Close	MF
1	49.25	
2	49.75	
3	50.25	+1.00
4	50.75	+1.00
5	51.10	+ .85
6	50.75	0
7	51.00	— .10
8	49.75	—1.00
9	49.25	—1.75
10	49.50	— .25

In this example, the first momentum factor (MF) was obtained by subtracting 49.25 (Day 1) from 50.25 (Day 3). The second MF was obtained by subtracting Day 2 from Day 4. The third was obtained by subtracting Day 3 from Day 5.

Now let's look at Day 7. We subtract 51.10 from 51.00 and get a minus .10 (—.10). Whenever we subtract a larger number from a smaller number, we always use the sign of the number being subtracted. In this case, it is the sign of the larger number. On Day 9, 49.25 minus 51.00 gives a difference of —1.75.

Below is a graphic example of the procedure:

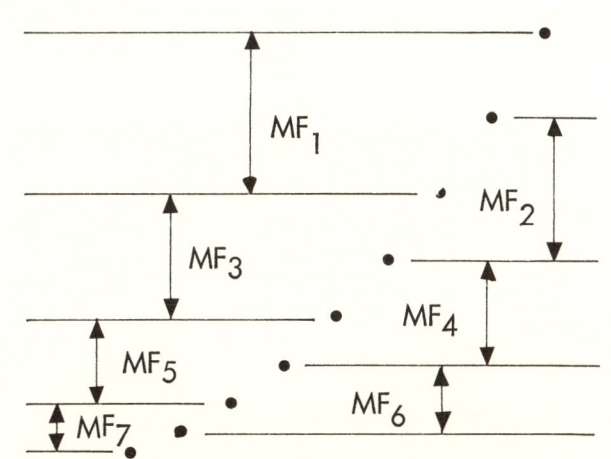

Fig. 5.2 (illustrates acceleration)

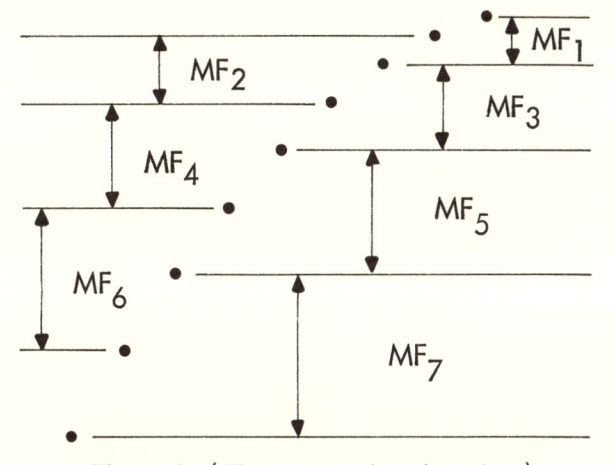

Fig. 5.3 (illustrates deceleration)

Now that we know how to determine the momentum factor on a daily basis, at this point we will outline the overall concept of the trading procedure and then take it step by step.

BASIC PROCEDURE

(1) Go *Long* on the close today when the momentum factor today is a higher number than the momentum factor for **either** of the previous two days.

(2) Go *Short* on the close today when today's momentum factor is a lower number than the momentum factor for **both** of the previous two days.

(3) Take profits at the target. Do not reverse.

(4) Exit the market at the STOP. Do not reverse.

(5) When **out** of the market, either at the target or at the stop, reenter on the close under the first or second procedure as applicable.

Let's look again at our example:

Day	Close	MF	Position	Price
1	49.25			
2	49.75			
3	50.25	+1.00		
4	50.75	+1.00		
5	51.10	+ .85	Short	51.10
6	50.75	0		
7	51.00	— .10		
8	49.75	—1.00		
9	49.25	—1.75		
10	49.50	— .25	Long	49.50

We went *Short* on the close on Day 5 because the MF of +.85 was a lower number than both of the two previous momentum factors. If the MF on Day 5 had been lower than **only one** of the two previous MF's, we would not have had a signal. **It must be lower than both of the two previous MF's to have a valid signal.** Once we are *Short*, we then calculate the target at which point we will take profits. But before we take up the target, let's continue the discussion of the entry point.

Now let's go back to Day 5. If you have followed the discussion to this point, you have one big question in mind. You have looked at the example and wondered, "If I have to know the close price before I can determine the momentum factor, how am I going to enter the market *Short* on the close at 51.10?" That's a good question. The answer is that we can determine before the close — in fact, even before the open on Day 5 — exactly what price will be necessary to produce a momentum factor of less than 1.00. This brings us to the TREND BALANCE POINT.

Since we are going to subtract Day 3 from Day 5 to obtain the momentum factor for Day 5, we can see very quickly that the close price of 51.25 on Day 5 will give an MF of +1.00. If the close is less than 51.25, the MF will be less than +1.00. If the close is higher than 51.25, we know the MF will be higher than +1.00. If the close is exactly 51.25, then the MF today will be equal to +1.00; therefore, 51.25 is a very crucial point. We call this point the TREND BALANCE POINT (TBP). If we are *Long* in the market, the TBP is defined as:

The point the price must close **below** in order to reverse our position to *Short*. If we are *Short* in the market, the TBP is defined as:

The point the price must close **above** in order to reverse our position to *Long*.

Here is our example again, with the TREND BALANCE POINTS indicated:

Day	Close	MF	TBP	Position	Price
1	49.25				
2	49.75				
3	50.25	+1.00			
4	50.75	+1.00			
5	51.10	+ .85	51.25	Short	51.10
6	50.75	0	51.75		
7	51.00	— .10	51.95		
8	49.75	—1.00	50.75		
9	49.25	—1.75	50.90		
10	49.50	— .25	48.75	Long	49.50
11			47.50		

On Day 5, the TBP was 51.25; therefore, we went *Short* on the close at 51.10. As soon as the market closes on Day 5, we can calculate the TBP for the following day. The question is, how high can the market close the following day and not produce an MF which will be higher than 1.00? Since the MF must be higher than both of the two previous momentum factors, obviously we pick the **higher** of the two previous momentum factors. In this case, they are +1.00 and +.85. The higher of the two is +1.00. Since we are *Short* we pick the **higher** MF and add this number to the close on Day 4 and obtain a TBP of 51.95 to be used for Day 6. On Day 6, our

55

NEW CONCEPTS IN TECHNICAL TRADING SYSTEMS

previous two momentum factors are +.85 and 0. We pick the higher of these two, +.85, and add this number to the close on Day 5 and obtain a TBP of 51.95 to be used for Day 7. On Day 7, we look at the two previous momentum factors, which are 0 and —.10. **The higher of these two is 0;** therefore, we add 0 to the close on Day 6 and obtain a TBP of 50.75 to be used for Day 8. On Day 8, the higher of the two previous momentum factors is —.10. We add —.10 to the close on Day 7 and obtain a TBP of 50.90 to be used for Day 9

Remember, if we add a minus number to a plus number, the answer is the **difference** between the two numbers.

Now suppose we had taken profits at the *Short* trade target on Day 10. How would we reenter the market on the close of Day 10 — *Long* or *Short*? Since we had already calculated the TBP to be 48.75, we will go *Long* if the close is **above** 48.75 and *Short* if the close is **at or below** 48.75. Since we were *Short*, we would not change direction if the close were exactly 48.75. Whenever the close is exactly equal to the TBP, we continue to trade in the same direction.

Notice that —.25 is a higher number than the two previous momentum factors which are —1.00 and —1.75. (If operating with minus numbers is a little confusing at first, think of it this way; —25° is a higher temperature than —100° or —175°.)

Now that we are *Long*, to obtain the TREND BALANCE POINT, the question is, what close price will produce an MF **lower** than the two previous momentum factors? Now we take the **lower** of the two previous momentum factors and add this number to the close two days ago in order to obtain the TBP for the following day.

On Day 11, the two previous momentum factors are —1.75 and —.25. The lower of these two is —1.75; therefore, we add —1.75 to 49.25 and obtain a TBP of 47.50. So, at the end of trading on Day 10, we know that on Day 11 we will maintain our *Long* position unless the close that day is **lower** than 47.50, at which point we will reverse to *Short*.

Now let's review the procedure for obtaining the TREND BALANCE POINT (TBP):

(1) To obtain the TBP for tomorrow if *Long*, select the **lower** of the two previous momentum factors and add this number to yesterday's close.

(2) To obtain the TBP for tomorrow if *Short*, select the **higher** of the two previous momentum factors and add this number to yesterday's close.

NOTE: the two previous momentum factors are the MF for today and the MF for yesterday.

When stated in this manner it becomes a very simple procedure.

Remember, when we add a minus number to a plus number, we take the difference and use the sign of the larger number. For instance, if we add an MF of —1.75 to a close price of 49.25, our answer will be 47.50.

PROTECTIVE STOP

At this point, we know when to enter and when to exit the market. Since we enter on the close, we need a **protective stop** for the next day in case of an extreme move and in case the price should close limit against us and lock us in the market. Our stop must also be relative to the momentum concept upon which the system is based.

The stop for this system is a function of the True Range (TR) and the Average Price ($\overline{X}$). The equation for the stop is $\overline{X}$ plus or minus TR. If we are *Long*, the equation is $\overline{X}$ — TR. If we are *Short*, the equation is $\overline{X}$ + TR. $\overline{X}$ is a simple average of the high, low and close price. It is obtained by adding the high, low and close and dividing by three.

The True Range, TR, is the same one-day True Range used in other systems in this book. To recap briefly, it is the **largest** of the following three possibilities:

(1) The distance between the high and low made during the day.

(2) The distance between today's high and yesterday's close, or
(3) The distance between today's low and yesterday's close.

Let's look at an example. Suppose the following prices are for the last two days of trading:

	High	Low	Close
Day 1	50.00	49.00	49.10
Day 2 (today)	50.20	49.40	49.90

High to low = .80

Previous close to today's high = 1.10

Previous close to today's low = .30

True Range = 1.10

$\overline{X}$ = 50.20 + 49.40 + 49.90 = 149.50 ÷ 3 = 49.83

If *Long*, the stop is $\overline{X}$ — TR.

49.83 — 1.10 = 48.73

If *Short*, the stop is $\overline{X}$ + TR.

49.83 + 1.10 = 50.93

The stop is calculated after the market closes, using the most recent high, low and close price, and is then for use on the **following day**.

TARGET

The Target for this system is a function of the Average Price, $\overline{X}$ and the extreme price made for the day. If we are *Long*, the equation for the Target is 2$\overline{X}$ — L. If we are *Short*, the equation for the Target is 2$\overline{X}$ — H. For example, suppose the following prices are for the last two days of trading:

	High	Low	Close
Day 1	50.00	49.00	49.10
Day 2 (today)	50.20	49.40	49.90

In the above example, if we were *Long*, the target for Day 3 would be:

$\overline{X}$ = 49.83
T = 2$\overline{X}$ — L
  = 2 x 49.83 — 49.40
  = 99.66 — 49.40
  = 50.26

If we were *Short*, the target for Day 3 would be:

T = 2$\overline{X}$ — H
  = 2 x 49.83 — 50.20
  = 99.66 — 50.20
    49.46

The target is calculated after the market closes, using the most recent high, low and close price, and is then for use on the **following day**.

We always put the Target, the Stop and the Trend Balance Point (TBP) on the line on the work sheet for the following day because they apply to the following day.

To recap briefly, a position is entered only on the close in accordance with the momentum factor. A position is exited at the target, but not reversed. If a position is exited during the day at the target, then the position is reinstated on the close as indicated by the TREND BALANCE POINT. The TBP also determines whether an **existing position** should be held or reversed on the close. If the position has been stopped out by the stop during the day, no reversal is made at the stop. The position is reinstated on the close in accordance with the TREND BALANCE POINT.

Following are the definitions and rules of the TREND BALANCE POINT SYSTEM.

DEFINITIONS — TREND BALANCE POINT SYSTEM

TR   TRUE RANGE: the greatest of:
- (1) The distance between today's high and low.
- (2) The distance between today's high and yesterday's close, or
- (3) The distance between today's low and yesterday's close.

MF   MOMENTUM FACTOR
Today's close minus the close the day before yesterday.

$\bar{X}$ $\bar{X}$ BAR
Today's high, low and close, added together and divided by three.

TBP   TREND BALANCE POINT:
- (1) If *Long*, the price at which the close must be **below** to reverse to *Short*.
- (2) If *Short*, the price at which the close must be **above** to reverse to *Long*.

STOP   STOP (Non-Reversing)
- (1) If *Long*, Stop is $\bar{X}$ minus True Range.
- (2) If *Short*, Stop is $\bar{X}$ plus True Range.

TARGET   TARGET (Exit only — Non-Reversing)
- (1) If *Long*, target is $2\bar{X} - L$.
- (2) If *Short*, target is $2\bar{X} - H$.

RULES — TREND BALANCE POINT SYSTEM

INITIAL ENTRY:

(1) Enter *Long* on **close** when close is **above** the Trend Balance Point.
(2) Enter *Short* on **close** when close is **below** the Trend Balance Point.

REVERSE ENTRY (if Target or Stop not touched):

(1) Reverse on **close** from *Short* to *Long* when close is **above** the Trend Balance Point.
(2) Reverse on **close** from *Long* to *Short* when close is **below** the Trend Balance Point.

EXIT:

(1) Exit position at Target. Do not reverse.
(2) Exit position at Stop. Do not reverse.

RE-ENTRY:

(1) Re-enter on close as dictated by the Trend Balance Point after exiting at Stop or at Target.

DETERMINATION OF TREND BALANCE POINT FOR TOMORROW:

(1) If *Long* select the **lower** of the two previous momentum factors and add this number to yesterday's close.
(2) If *Short* select the **higher** of the two previous momentum factors and add the number to yesterday's close.

An optional way to trade this system is to reinstate the position on the **open** the following day rather than on the close the previous day. Although I have obtained better overall results in trading this system by reinstating a position on the close, some traders may prefer to eliminate the risk of an overnight position and also obtain the reduced day trading commission by reinstating on the open. If this option makes you feel more comfortable, then by all means, tailor the system to suit your trading disposition. I would certainly recommend taking this option on any day that a significant FDA or other major report is coming out on the commodity you are following.

Now let's look quickly at some pecularities of this system. Compared to the stop, the target is relatively close. This is just the opposite of most systems which have a close stop and a long target. This concept is probably contrary to anything you have read, yet when you think it through, this concept becomes very interesting. First of all, the momentum factor keeps the trader in the market in the direction of the momentum so you have a definite edge in the direction you are trading; therefore the chances of reaching a relatively close target before reacting to a longer stop are decidedly in the trader's favor. The Trend Balance Point also acts as a stop. If the trade is not going in your direction the position will usually be reversed on the close in accordance with the TBP long before the stop is touched. Most traders have experienced the frustration of using very close stops and being continually stopped out. They then realize that all these small losses often consume — and sometimes exceed — the occasional large profit. It's not unusual for this system to show between 70% and 80% profit trades.

I know traders who can never seem to hang on and follow a good system because of a compulsive need for action. I know other traders who have a greater need to be right most of the time than they have a need for the money they can make. So, if you have a method that makes money over a long term and has proved itself successful for you, then stay with it. But, in the meantime, if you need action and are not trying to make a killing on every trade, this little system could be beneficial in more ways than one.

The trader does not have to be overly concerned about how many others are trading this system. Most of the time the price will hit the target. If there are a large number of orders at this point and the market "runs" these stops, then any slippage will be in the trader's favor.

There is always a large volume of 'on close only' orders in the market, so a few more will make relatively little difference.

The stop is seldom touched; however, to insure that a number of stop orders do not accumulate at one price, the trader can use a constant multiplier between .90 and 1.00 of the True Range and use this new value for the True Range in calculating the Stop.

Following is a work sheet example of this system on March 1978 Plywood.

WORK SHEET EXPLANATION

8/19/77	We go *Short* on the close at 210.80 because the close is below the TBP of 217.20.
8/22/77	The target of 208.54 was not hit and since the close is still below the TBP of 214.50, we hold the position.
8/23/77	We take profits at the target of 208.00 and reinstate the *Short* position on the close because the close is below the TBP of 209.80.
8/24/77	We take profits at the target of 200.50 and reinstate the *Short* position on the close, which is still below the TBP.
8/25/77	We take profits at the target of 197.80. The close of 196.30 is above the TBP, so we go *Long* on the close.
8/26/77	We take profits at the target of 200.86 (200.90) and reinstate the *Long* position on the close, which is above the TBP.
8/29/77	We take profits at the target of 202.66 (202.70) and again reinstate the *Long* position on the close. To break the monotony, let's skip down to a loss trade . . .
9/1/77	We go *Short* on the close at 202.30 which is below the TBP.
9/2/77	Neither the target nor the stop is touched, so we remain in the *Short* trade as determined by the close, which is below the TBP.
9/6/77	Again, neither the target nor the stop is reached; however, we reverse to *Long* on the close at 205.50, which is now above the TBP.
9/7/77	Our target of 208.50 is reached and we are back in the profit column again. The *Long* position is reinstated on the close at 208.50.

DAILY WORK SHEET

TREND BALANCE POINT SYSTEM

DATE	OPEN	HIGH	LOW	CLOSE	MF	TR	$\bar{X}$	TBP	$\bar{X}$ - TR LG STOP
8-15-77 M	206.50	207.80	206.20	206.80					
16	206.80	208	206.30	206.50		1.70			
17	208.40	212.50	208.40	212.	+5.20	6.00			
18	211	212.50	210	210.50	+4.00	2.50	211.		
19	211	212	208	210.80	-1.20	4.00	210.27	217.20	
22 M	211	213	209	209.50	-1.00	4.00	210.50	214.50	
23	208.50	208.50	202.50	202.50	-8.30	7.00	204.50	209.80	
24	202	204	195.80	203	-6.50	8.20	200.93	208.50	
25	203	203	196	196.30	-6.20	7.00	198.43	196.	
26	195.50	202	195	199.50	-3.50	7.00	198.83	196.50	191.43
29 M	200	206.50	200	206	9.70	7.00	204.17	190.10	191.83
30	206	209	206	208.80	9.30	3.00	207.93	196	197.17
31	210.40	210.90	209	209.30	3.30	2.10	209.73	215.30	204.93
9-1-77	209.30	209.30	202.30	202.30	-6.50	7.00	204.63	218.10	
2	201.50	205.40	201.30	205.20	-4.10	4.10	203.97	212.60	
5 M	HOLIDAY								
6	206.50	207	205	205.50	3.20	2.00	205.83	198.20	
7	206	209.20	205.20	208.50	3.30	4.00	207.63	201.10	203.83
8	209.50	211	206.50	206.70	1.20	4.50	208.07	208.70	203.63
9	206	208	205	206.50	-2.00	3.00	206.50	211.80	
12 M	207.20	208.20	206	206.80	.10	2.20	207.00	207.90	
13	206.50	206.50	201.50	201.50	-5.00	5.30	203.17	206.60	
14	201.50	204.20	200.50	203	-3.80	1.50	203.00	206.90	
15	203.	203.30	200.80	203.20	1.70	2.50	202.43	197.70	
16	203.50	204	202	202.70	-.30	2.00	202.90	199.20	199.93
19 M	201	201	198.70	198.80	-4.40	4.00	199.50	202.90	200.90
20	201.60	201.60	198.60	200	-2.70	3.00	200.07	202.40	
21	200.50	201.30	199.20	200.60	1.80	2.10	200.37	196.10	
22	200	200	198.50	198.90	-1.10	2.10	199.13	197.30	198.27
23	199.50	201.80	196.50	201.50	.90	5.30	199.93	199.50	197.03
26 M	201	203	201	201.50	2.60	2.00	201.83	197.80	194.63
27	201.80	206	201	206	4.50	5.00	204.33	202.40	199.83
28	206	206.30	203.80	204.30	2.80	2.50	204.80	204.10	199.33
29	204.10	205.30	203	205.20	-.80	2.30	204.50	208.80	202.30
30	205.50	206.30	203.60	203.80	-.50	2.70	204.57	207.10	
10-3-77 M	205.30	209.50	205.20	209	3.80	5.70	207.90	204.70	
4	208.80	210.80	208.10	208.10	4.30	2.70	209.00	203.30	202.20
5	208.50	209.90	208.50	209.50	.50	1.80	209.30	212.80	206.30
6	210.50	213.90	210.20	213.40	6.30	4.40	212.50	212.40	211.10
7	213	213.20	209.60	211.40	1.90	3.80	211.40	210	208.10
10 M	211.40	211.50	208.70	208.90	-4.50	2.80	209.70	215.30	207.60
11	208.50	211	207.50	208.10	-3.30	3.50	208.87	213.30	
12	207.80	208	203	203.50	-5.40	5.10	204.83	205.60	
13	202	203	199	199.10	-9.00	4.50	200.37	204.80	
14	198	202	197	201.60				198.10	195.87

61

COMMODITY **Plywood**   CONTRACT MONTH **March 1978**

X̄−L TARGET	X̄+TR ST STOP	2X̄−H ST TARGET	ENTRY	EXIT	
	213.50	209.50	S-210.80		
	214.27	208.54	HOLD		
	214.50	208.	S-202.50	208.	+2.80
	211.50	200.50	S-203	200.50	+2.00
	209.13	197.86	L-196.30	197.80	+5.20
0.86			L-199.50	200.90	+4.60
2.66			L-206	202.70	+3.20
8.34			L-208.80	208.40	+2.40
9.86			S-209.30	210.40	+1.60
	211.83	208.56	S-202.30	208.50	+1.40
	211.63	199.96	HOLD		
	208.07	202.54	L-205.50	205.50	−3.20
6.66			L-208.50	206.70	+1.20
0.06			S-206.70	210.10	+1.60
	212.57	205.14	S-206.50	205.10	+1.60
	209.50	205.00	HOLD		
	209.20	205.80	S-201.50	205.80	+.70
	208.47	199.84	HOLD		
	206.27	200.90	L-203.20	200.90	+.60
4.04			L-202.70	204	+.80
3.80			S-198.80	200.90	−1.80
	203.50	198.00	HOLD		
	203.07	198.54	L-200.60	200.60	−1.80
1.54			HOLD		
9.16			L-201.50	199.80	−.80
3.36			HOLD		
2.66			L-206	202.70	+1.20
7.66			HOLD		
5.80			S-205.20	205.20	−.80
	206.80	203.70	S-203.80	203.70	+1.50
	207.27	202.84	L-209	207.30	−3.50
0.60			L-208.10	210.60	+1.60
9.90			S-209.50	209.90	+1.80
8.70			L-213.40	211.10	−1.60
4.80			HOLD		
3.20			S-208.90	208.90	−4.50
	212.50	207.90	S-208.10	207.90	+1.00
	212.37	206.74	S-203.50	206.70	+1.40
	209.93	201.66	L-199.10	201.60	+1.90
1.74	204.87	197.74		197.70	+1.40

62

SECTION VI

THE RELATIVE STRENGTH INDEX

The RELATIVE STRENGTH INDEX, RSI, is a tool which can add a new dimension to chart interpretation when plotted in conjunction with a daily bar chart. Some of these interpretative factors are:

TOPS and BOTTOMS are indicated when the RSI goes above 70 or drops below 30.

CHART FORMATIONS which often show up graphically on the RSI may not be apparent on the bar chart.

FAILURE SWINGS above 70 or below 30 on the RSI scale are strong indications of market reversals.

SUPPORT and RESISTANCE often show up clearly on the RSI before becoming apparent on the bar chart.

DIVERGENCE between the RSI and price action on the chart is a very strong indication that a market turning point is imminent.

Before taking up the equation for calculating the Relative Strength Index, let's examine briefly the momentum concept upon which the RSI is based.

The Momentum Oscillator Concept

One of the most useful tools employed by many technicians is the momentum oscillator. The momentum oscillator measures the velocity of directional price movement. When the price moves up very rapidly, at some point it is considered to be overbought; when it moves down very rapidly, at some point it is considered to be oversold. In either case, a reaction or reversal is imminent. The slope of the momentum oscillator is directly proportional to the velocity of the move. The distance traveled up or down by the momentum oscillator is proportional to the magnitude of the move.

The momentum oscillator is usually characterized by a line on a chart drawn in two dimensions. The 'Y' axis (vertical) represents magnitude or distance the indicator moves; the 'X' axis (horizontal) represents time. The momentum oscillator drawn in this manner is characterized by the fact that it moves very rapidly at market turning points and tends to slow down as the market continues the directional move.

Suppose we are using the close price to calculate the oscillator and the price is moving up daily by exactly the same increment from close to close. At some point, the oscillator begins to flatten out and eventually becomes a horizontal line. When this occurs, if the price begins to level out, the oscillator will begin to descend.

Let's look at this concept using a simple oscillator expressed in terms of the price today minus the price 'x' number of days ago. In this example, we will use the price today minus the price ten days ago. The oscillator is measured from a zero line. If the price ten days ago were higher than the price today, then the oscillator value is minus; conversely, if today's price were higher than the price ten days ago, then the oscillator value is plus.

The easiest way to illustrate the interaction between price movement and oscillator movement is to take a straight line-price relationship and plot the oscillator points based on this relationship.

In Fig. 6.1, we begin on Day 10 when the close price is 48.50. The price ten days ago, on Day 1, is 50.75. Utilizing a ten day oscillator, we take today's price of 48.50, subtract the price ten days ago, 50.75, and the result, —2.25, is the oscillator value. This oscillator value of —2.25 is plotted below the zero line. By following this

Fig. 6.1

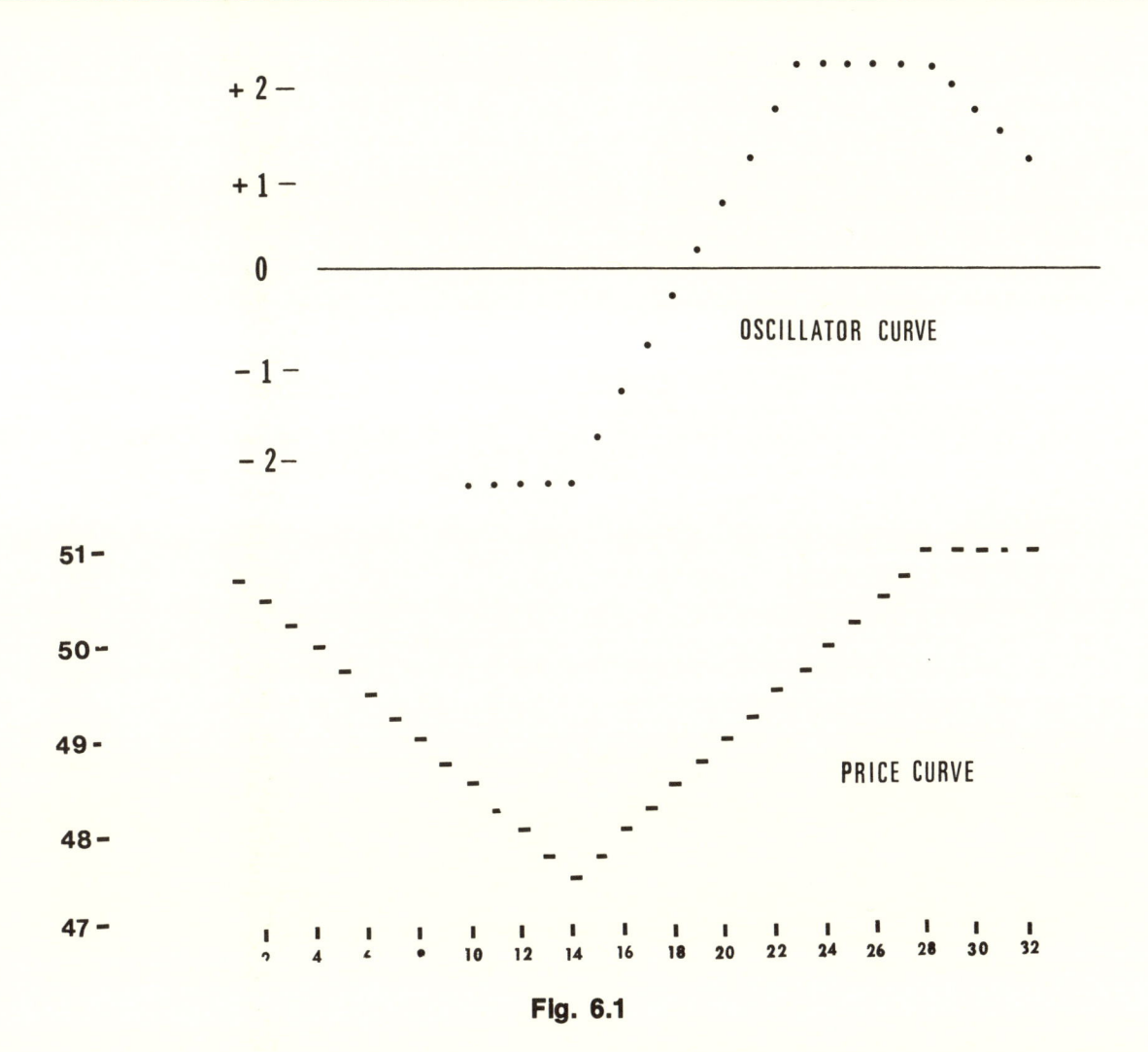

procedure for each day, we develop the oscillator curve.

The oscillator curve developed in this hypothetical situation is very interesting. As the price moves down by the same increment each day between Days 10 and 14, the oscillator curve is a horizontal line. On Day 15, the price turns up by 25 points yet the oscillator turns up by 50 points. The oscillator is increasing twice as fast as the price. The oscillator continues this rate of movement until Day 23 when its value becomes a constant although the price continues to move up at the same rate.

On Day 29, another very interesting thing happens. The price levels out at 51.00, yet the oscillator begins to go down, If the price continues to move horizontally, the oscillator will continue to descend until the tenth day at which time both the oscillator and the price will be moving horizontally.

Note the interaction of the oscillator curve and the price curve. The oscillator appears to be one step ahead of the price; the reason being that the oscillator, in effect, is measuring the **rate of change** of price movement. Between Days 14 and 23, the oscillator shows that the price rate of change is very fast because the direction of the price is changing from down to up. Once the price of ten days ago has bottomed out and started up, then the rate of change slows down because the increments of change are measured in one direction only.

The oscillator can be an excellent technical tool for the trader who understands its inherent characteristics; however, there are three problems encountered in developing a meaningful oscillator.

The first problem is erratic movement within the general oscillator configuration. As an example of this, using a ten day oscillator, suppose that ten days ago the price moved limit down from the previous day. Now, suppose that today, the price closed the same as yesterday. When we subtract the price ten days ago from the price today, we will get an erroneously high value for the oscillator today. To overcome this problem, there must be some way to dampen or smooth out the extreme points used to calculate the oscillator.

The second problem characteristic of oscillators is the scale to use for the 'Y' axis. In other words, how high is high and how low is low? The scale will also change with each commodity being charted. To overcome this problem, there must be some common denominator to apply to all commodities so the amplitude of the oscillator is relative and meaningful.

The third problem is the necessity of having to keep up with enormous amounts of data. This is the least of the three problems; however, it can become burdensome to the trader who is following several commodities with an oscillator technique.

The solution to these three problems is incorporated in the indicator which we will call THE RELATIVE STRENGTH INDEX.

The Relative Strength Index Equation

The equation for the Relative Strength Index, RSI, is:

$$RSI = 100 - \left[\frac{100}{1 + RS} \right]$$

$$RS = \frac{\text{Average of 14 day's closes UP}}{\text{Average of 14 day's closes DOWN}}$$

For the first calculation of the Relative Strength Index, RSI, we need the previous 14 day's close prices. From then on, we need only the previous day's data. The initial RSI is calculated as follows:

(1) Obtain the sum of the UP closes for the previous 14 days and divide this sum by 14. This is the **average** UP close.

(2) Obtain the sum of the DOWN closes for the previous 14 days and divide this sum by 14. This is the **average** DOWN close.

(3) Divide the **average** UP close by the **average** DOWN close. This is the Relative Strength (RS).

(4) Add 1.00 to the RS.

(5) Divide the result obtained in Step 4 **into** 100.

(6) Subtract the result obtained in Step 5 **from** 100. This is the **first** RSI.

From this point on, it is only necessary to use the previous **average** UP close and the previous **average** DOWN close in the calculation of the next RSI. This procedure, which incorporates the dampening or smoothing factor into the equation, is as follows:

(1) To obtain the next average UP close: Multiply the previous average UP close by 13, add to this amount today's UP close (if any) and divide the total by 14.

(2) To obtain the next average DOWN close: Multiply the previous average DOWN close by 13, add to this amount today's DOWN close (if any) and divide the total by 14.

Steps (3), (4), (5) and (6) are the same as for the initial RSI.

An easy way to keep up with the RSI on a daily basis is to use a ten column worksheet, Fig. 6.2.

Column #1 is the date.

Column #2 is the close price for the day.

Column #3 is the amount the price closed UP from the previous day.
(For example, on Day 2, the price closed UP 2.00 from Day 1. Entry is made in Column #3 **only** if the price closed UP from the previous day.)

Column #4 is the amount the price closed DOWN from the previous day.
(For example, on Day 8, the price closed DOWN 1.57 from the close on Day 7. Entry is made in column #4

DAILY WORK SHEET
RELATIVE STRENGTH INDEX

COMMODITY _____

CONTRACT MONTH _____

(1) DATE	(2) CLOSE	(3) UP	(4) DOWN	(5) UP AVG	(6) DOWN AVG	(7) (5) − (6)	(8) 1 + (7)	(9) 100 ÷ (8)	(10) 100 − (9)
1	54.80								
2	56.80	2.00							
3	57.85	1.05							
4	59.85	2.00							
5	60.57	.72							
6	61.10	.53							
7	62.17	1.07							
8	60.60		1.57						
9	62.35	1.75							
10	62.15		.20						
11	62.35	.20							
12	61.45		.90						
13	62.80	1.35							
14	61.37		1.43						
15	62.50	1.13 / 11.80	/ 4.10	.84	.29	2.90	3.90	25.64	74.36
16	62.57	.07		.79	.27	2.93	3.93	25.45	74.55
17	60.80		1.77	.73	.38	1.92	2.92	34.25	65.75
18	59.37		1.43	.68	.46	1.48	2.48	40.32	59.68
19	60.35	.98		.70	.43	1.63	2.63	38.02	61.98
20	62.35	2.00		.79	.40	1.98	2.98	33.56	66.44
21	62.17		.18	.73	.38	1.92	2.92	34.25	65.75
22	62.55	.38		.71	.35	2.03	3.03	33.00	67.00
23	64.55	2.00		.80	.32	2.50	3.50	28.57	71.43
24	64.37		.18	.74	.31	2.39	3.39	29.50	70.50
25	65.30	.93		.75	.29	2.59	3.59	27.86	72.14
26	64.42		.88	.70	.33	2.12	3.12	32.05	67.95
27	62.90		1.52	.65	.42	1.55	2.55	39.22	60.78
28	61.60		1.30	.60	.48	1.25	2.25	44.44	55.56
29	62.05	.45		.59	.45	1.31	2.31	43.29	56.71
30	60.05		2.00	.55	.56	.98	1.98	50.51	49.49
31	59.70		.35	.51	.55	.93	1.93	51.81	48.19
32	60.90	1.20		.56	.51	1.10	2.10	47.62	52.38
33	60.25		.65	.52	.52	1.00	2.00	50.00	50.00
34	58.27		1.98	.48	.62	.77	1.77	56.50	43.50
35	58.70	.43		.48	.58	.83	1.83	54.64	45.36
36	57.72		.98	.45	.61	.74	1.74	57.47	42.53
37	58.10	.38		.45	.57	.79	1.79	55.87	44.13
38	58.20	.10		.43	.53	.81	1.81	55.25	44.75

Fig. 6.2

only of the price closed DOWN from the previous day.)

Column #5 is the value of the average UP close. (On Day 15, we have the necessary information to begin calculating the RSI. We add all the values in Column #3 and obtain a sum of 11.80. We then divide this sum by 14 to obtain the **average** UP close for the 14-day period. This value of .84 is put in Column #5.)

Column #6 is the value of the average DOWN close.
(Sum the DOWN closes in Column #4 and obtain 4.10. Divide this figure by 14 and obtain the **average** DOWN close and put this value of .29 in Column #6.)

Column #7 is the **result** of dividing the number in Column #5 by the number in Column #6.
(.84 ÷ .29 = 2.90)

Column #8 is the **result** of adding 1.00 to the number in Column #7.
(2.90 + 1.00 = 3.90)

Column #9 is the **result** of dividing 100 by the number in Column #8.
(100 ÷ 3.90 = 25.64)

Column #10 is the value of the Relative Strength Index and is derived by subtracting the number in Column #9 **from** 100.
(100 — 25.64 = 74.36)

On Day 16 and thereafter, we are no longer concerned with data for the previous 14 days. The RSI is calculated using only the previous day's average UP close and average DOWN close. The procedure for obtaining the average UP and DOWN closes is as follows:

On Day 16, take the previous average UP close in Column #5, which is .84 and multiply it by 13. Add to this the UP close for the day (in Column #3) and divide the total by 14.

.84 x 13 = 10.92
+ .07
10.99 ÷ 14 = .79

The result, .79, is the **new** average Up close and is placed in Column #5.

Since the price on Day 16 closed up, the value of the average DOWN close must **decrease** relative to the 14 day average. However, the procedure is the same. Take the average DOWN close in Column #6, which is .29, multiply this by 13. Since the down close on Day 16 was zero, there is nothing to add back. Now divide the total by 14.

.29 × 13 = 3.77
+ 0
3.77 ÷ 14 = .27

Columns #7 through #10 are filled in as explained previously.

Now that we know how to obtain the RELATIVE STRENGTH INDEX number for each day, let's discuss briefly the peculiarities of the RSI in light of the three problems inherent to most oscillators:

(1) Erroneous erratic movement is eliminated by the averaging technique. However, the RSI is amply responsive to price movement because an increase of the average close UP is automatically coordinated with a decrease in the average close DOWN and vice versa.

(2) The question of 'how high is high and how low is low' is answered because the RSI value must always fall between 0 and 100. Therefore, the daily momentum of any number of commodities can be measured on the same scale for comparison to each other and to previous highs and lows within the same commodity. The most active commodities are those in which the RSI is showing the greatest vertical movement — either up or down.

(3) The problem of having to keep up with mountains of previous data is also solved. After calculating the initial RSI, only the previous day's data is required for the next calculation.

Learning to use this index is a lot like learning to read a chart. The more a trader studies the interaction between chart movement and the Relative Strength Index, the more revealing the RSI will become. If used properly, the RSI can be a very valuable tool in interpreting chart movement. The RSI points are plotted daily on a bar chart and when connected, form the RSI line.

Now let's look at the different things this index can tell us; first, the Index itself indicates:

(1) **Tops and Bottoms:** These are indicated when the Index goes above 70 or below 30. The Index will usually top out or bottom out before the actual market top or bottom, giving an indication that a reversal or at least a significant reaction is imminent.

(2) **Chart Formations:** The Index will display graphic chart formations which may not be obvious on a corresponding bar chart. For instance, head and shoulders tops or bottoms, pennants or triangles often show up on the Index to indicate breakouts and buy and sell points.

(3) **Failure Swings:** Failure swings above 70 or below 30 are very strong indications of a market reversal. (See Fig. 6.3 and Fig. 6.4.)

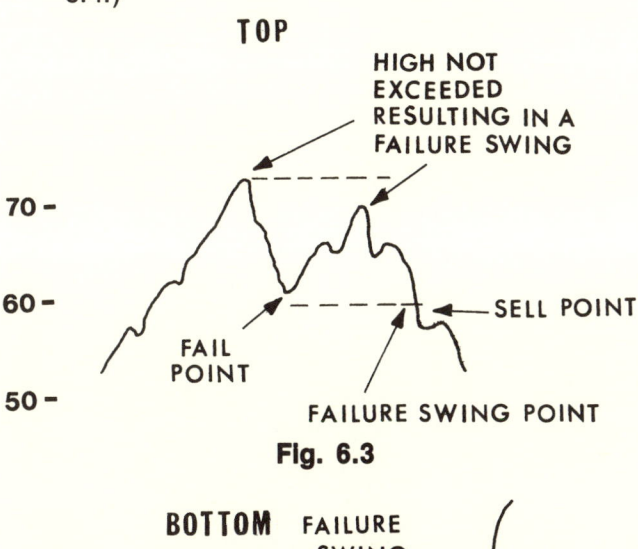

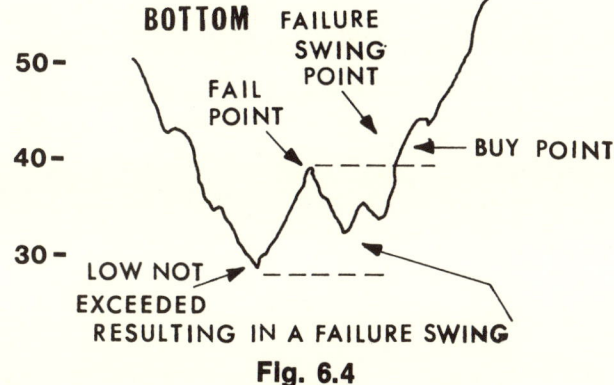

TOP

Fig. 6.3

BOTTOM

Fig. 6.4

Second, the Index, in conjunction with the bar chart, defines these interactions:

(4) **Support and Resistance:** Areas of support and resistance often show up clearly on the Index before becoming apparent on the bar chart. In fact, support and resistance lines drawn using Index points are often analogous to trend lines drawn using bar chart points.

(5) **Divergence:** Divergence between price action and the RSI is a very strong indicator of a market turning point. Divergence occurs when the RSI is increasing and the price movement is either flat or decreasing. Conversely, divergence occurs when the RSI is decreasing and price movement is either flat or increasing. (Note on the June Silver chart, Fig. 6.5, that there was divergence between the bar chart and the RSI at every major turning point.)

In view of these five interpretive factors of the RSI, let's examine the bar chart of June 1978 Chicago Silver.

(1) **Tops and bottoms:** The major bottom of August 15 was accompanied by an RSI value below 30. During the next few days, a turning point was indicated by divergence between the RSI and price action. The major top of November 9 was preceded by an RSI value above 70. The top made on January 24 was preceded by an RSI value of less than 70. This would indicate that this top is less significant than the previous one and that either a higher top is in the making or that the long-term up trend is running out of steam.

(2) **Chart Formation:** Note the pennant formed on the RSI line during October that is not evident on the bar chart. A breakout of this triangle indicates an intermediate move in the direction of the breakout. Note also the long-term pennant with the large number of supporting points on the RSI line. A significant breakout of this triangle should be indicative of the next long-term trend.

(3) **Failure Swings:** Failure swings made by this Index are most significant after an RSI high in the area of 70 or low in the area of 30. Note that when the RSI reached 70, the immediate down swing carried to 58. It is not un-

CONTRACT SIM 78
HIGH 536.60:03/21/77
LOW 454.00: 08/23/77
AS OF THURS.
COMMODITY PERSPECTIVE • 327 S. LaSalle • Chicago, Illinois 60604
CHICAGO SILVER
JUNE
Chicago Board of Trade
CENTS PER TROY OZ.
(GRID VALUE= 0.5)
530
525
520
515
510
505
500
495
490
485
480
475
470
465
460
455
450
D = DIVERGENCE
D_1
D_2
D_3
D_4
80
70
60
50
40
30
JULY
AUG
SEPT
OCT
NOV
DEC
JAN.
FEB.
MAR.

usual for the following up swing to be composed of several small swings as long as the high and low of the main swing are not penetrated. When the low point of 58 was penetrated, the failure swing was completed. On the low of August 15, the failure swing carried up to 41 on the RSI scale. After several small down swings, this point was penetrated on the up side on August 26.

(4) **Support and Resistance:** Trend lines on the bar chart often show up as support lines on the RSI. Notice the support lines made by the low swing points during October and part of November could be used to confirm trend lines drawn on the chart. Depending upon who is drawing the trend line, a breaking of the trend line could have occurred on November 4; however, this was not confirmed on the support line drawn on the RSI.

(5) **Divergence:** Although divergence does not occur at every turning point, it does occur at most significant turning points. When divergence begins to show up after a good directional move, this is a very strong indication that a turning point is near. Divergence is the single most indicative characteristic of the Relative Strength Index. Note that the top made on November 9 was **indicated** by an RSI value above 70 and divergence. It was **confirmed** by the failure swing, breaking out of the pennant formation and breaking the support line.

The Relative Strength Index, used in conjunction with a bar chart, can provide a new dimension of interpretation for the chart reader. No single tool, method or system is going to produce the right answers 100% of the time. A successful trader utilizes several different kinds of input into his decisions. Often the problem is in narrowing this input down to two or three things that work best for him. In this context, the Relative Strength Index can be a valuable input into this decision-making process.

SECTION VII

THE REACTION TREND SYSTEM

The Reaction Trend System is just what the name implies — it is both an anti-trend system and a trend system. The normal mode of operation is the REACTION MODE (anti-trend). In the REACTION MODE, we buy on weakness and sell on strength. The anti-trend mode reverses at each buy point and most sell points. The TREND MODE of the system does not reverse, but exits the market at a trailing stop.

This system provides plenty of action. It will average making a trade about every two or three days. This system capitalizes on the kind of market most systems perform very poorly in; that is, those exasperating markets which have periods of non-directional congestion-type action and suddenly spurt to new highs or new lows. These markets will show up on the lower end of the Directional Movement Index scale.

Characteristically, this system makes money in a non-directional market; however, when the market suddenly becomes directional and moves rapidly, it will automatically go into its TREND MODE and follow the move. When the trend halts, the system reverts to the anti-trend or REACTION MODE.

Before we get into the rules for trading, let's look at the geometry of the system in order to understand the concept upon which the price action points are based. The high, low and close prices for each day generate FOUR PRICE ACTION POINTS for the following day. **These points are good for the following day only.** The four price action points are all based on the **average** of the high, low and close price for the day which is designated $\overline{X}$.

$$\overline{X} = \frac{H + L + C}{3}$$

The four price action points are:

(1) B_1 (Buy Point) = $2\overline{X} - H$
(2) S_1 (Sell Point) = $2\overline{X} - L$
(3) HBOP (High Break Out Point) = $2\overline{X} - 2L + H$
(4) LBOP (Low Break Out Point) = $2\overline{X} - 2H + L$

The geometry for these points is diagrammed in Fig. 7.1

All of the points are generated by three distances, D_1, D_2 and D_3.

(1) D_1 is the distance from $\overline{X}$ to the high price of the day. The BUY POINT, B_1, is obtained by swinging D_1 through an 180° arc below $\overline{X}$.

(2) D_2 is the distance between $\overline{X}$ and the low price of the day. The SELL POINT, S_1, is obtained by swinging D_2 through an 180° above $\overline{X}$.

(3) D_3 is the distance between the high and low of the day. The HIGH BREAK OUT POINT, HBOP, is the distance D_3 plus D_2 above $\overline{X}$.

The LOW BREAK OUT POINT, LBOP, is the distance D_3 plus D_1 below $\overline{X}$. The $\overline{X}$ is the base point for derivation of the equation of each of the four price action points which are shown in Fig. 7.1

Before we discuss **when** to take a position, let's look at the price action relative to the four price action points. We stated that the normal mode of operation for the Reaction Trend system is the REACTION mode. We also said that the four price action points generated on one day are good for the following day only. We are in the normal REACTION mode when the prices for the next day **stay within the bounds** of the HBOP and the LBOP. In this mode, we buy at point B_1 and sell at point S_1.

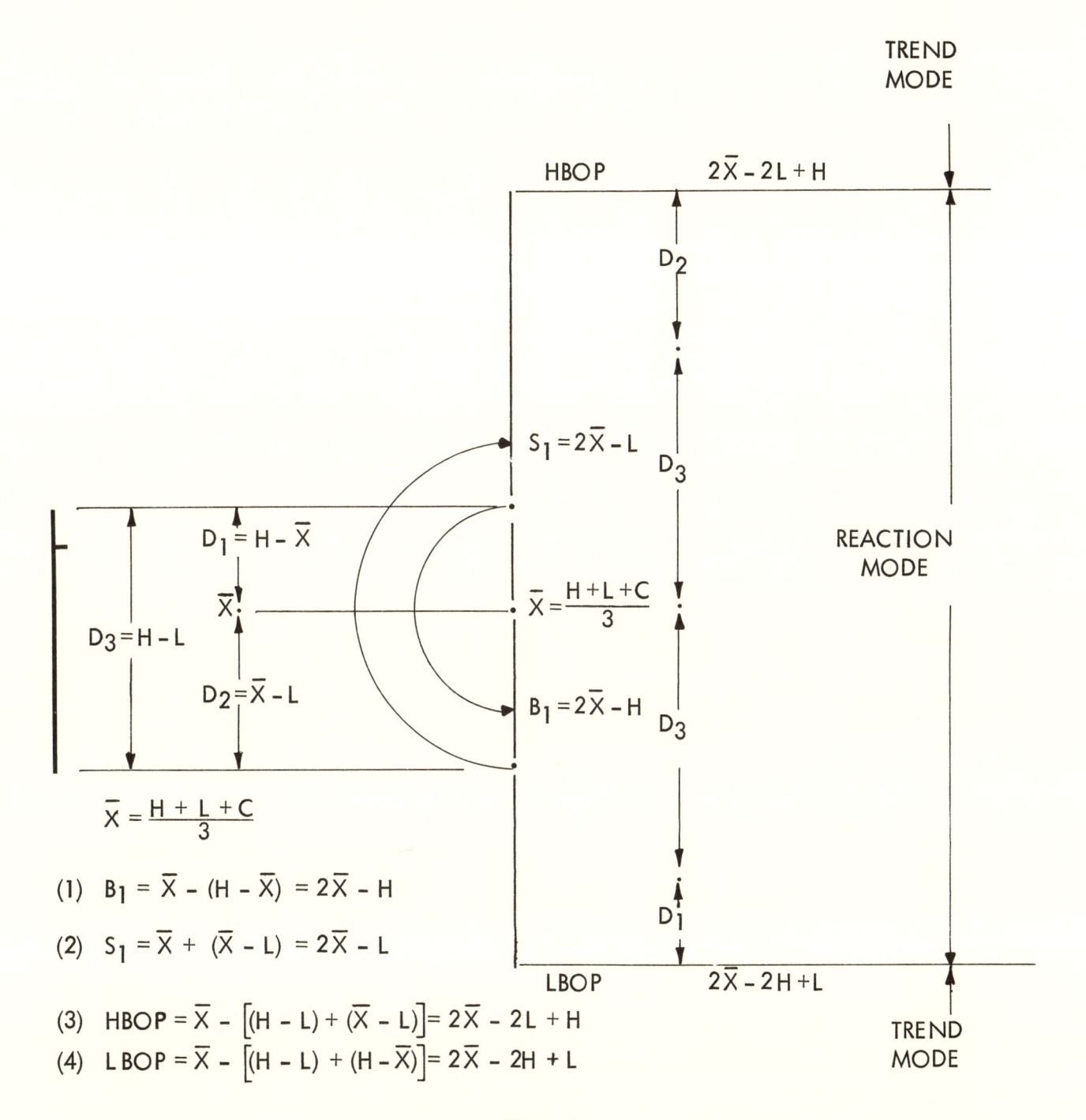

Fig. 7.1

$$\bar{X} = \frac{H+L+C}{3}$$

(1) $B_1 = \bar{X} - (H - \bar{X}) = 2\bar{X} - H$

(2) $S_1 = \bar{X} + (\bar{X} - L) = 2\bar{X} - L$

(3) $HBOP = \bar{X} - \left[(H-L) + (\bar{X} - L)\right] = 2\bar{X} - 2L + H$

(4) $LBOP = \bar{X} - \left[(H-L) + (H - \bar{X})\right] = 2\bar{X} - 2H + L$

If the price for the next day should **go through** the HBOP or the LBOP, the system is then automatically in TREND mode. Once in this mode, the stop becomes the most distant price of the previous two days. (If the price should go through the HBOP, the trailing stop is the lowest low made for the previous two days. If the price should go through the LBOP, the trailing stop is the highest high made for the previous two days.) We follow the price in the direction of the breakout with the trailing stop. When the price reacts enough after the breakout to trigger the trailing stop, we exit the market at the trailing stop. We then go back into the REACTION mode and remain until another breakout occurs.

This system is based on what appears to be a repetitious peculiarity of random price movement. This is the three-day-up-two-day-down phenomenon. This phenomenon is most prevalent in a non-directional market or a lazily trending market. For some reason, random price movement appears to take longer to increase than it does to decrease. This appears to be indicative of most price action; that is, the down moves are more severe and of shorter duration than the up moves. Often a good directional move starts with a significant increase in range on the first day of the move. When this happens, the breakout points will be exceeded and the system will go into TREND mode and follow the move until the first reaction occurs — at which time the system automatically reverts to the REACTION mode.

Now let's discuss the question of WHEN to enter the market. We look back over the price action for the last two or three weeks and select the **significantly lowest price** (Fig. 7.2).

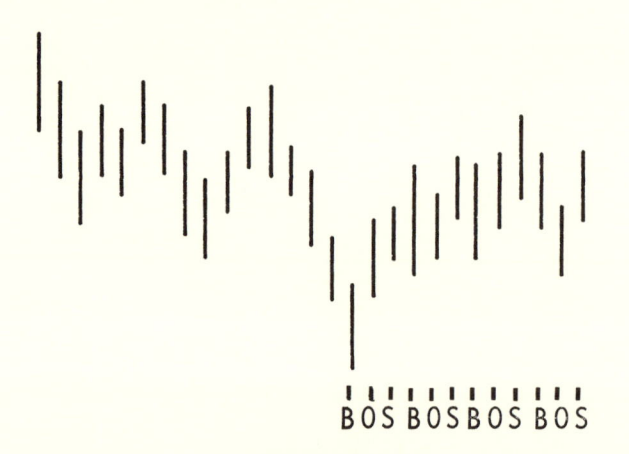

Fig. 7.2

We place a "B" under that day.

We place an "O" under the following day.

We place an "S" under the next day.

We designate all following days in the sequence, "B", "O", "S", "B", "O", "S", "B", "O", "S". (This represents nine days of the sequence.) We continue to designate all of the days in this sequence until we get to today.

If the market is in a general down trend, we can pick out the **significantly highest price** for the last two or three weeks and label the high point "S". The next day of the sequence would be "B", the following day, "O", etc.

An alternate method to begin the "B", "O", "S" sequence would be at a PHASING change or confirmation (after a breakout) which we will explain later.

Following are the **basic** principles for trading the REACTION TREND SYSTEM.

For trading the REACTION MODE:

(1) *Long* (BUY) positions are initiated **only** on a "B" day.
(2) *Short* (SELL) positions are initiated **only** on an "S" day.
(3) NO positions are initiated on an "O" day **except** those initaited by the breakout points, HBOP or LBOP.
(4) *Long* positions may be closed out on an "O" day or reversed on an "S" day.
(5) *Short* positions are reversed on a "B" day.
(6) The target and reverse point for a position initiated at B$_1$ is always S$_1$.
(7) The target and reverse point for a position initiated at S$_1$ is always B$_1$.

For trading the TREND MODE:

(1) Breakout points, HBOP and LBOP, are **stop and reversal** points for open positions in the Reaction Mode. They are also **entry** points for a new position. Any position initiated at HBOP or LBOP is taken on **any** day it occurs.
(2) The **stop** for any Trend Mode position is always the trailing stop. This Trailing Stop is **not** a reverse.

Now let's discuss how these rules are used. Assuming that we have designated our previous days as either "B", "O", or "S", we are ready to begin trading the Reaction Mode of this system. Suppose, however, that tomorrow is an "O" day. We cannot **initiate** a position on an "O" day, so we calculate the four price action points for the following "S" day. On the following "S" day, we can only go *Short*, and then **only** if the price touches the S$_1$ sell point. Assume that the price touched S$_1$ and we go *Short* (Fig. 7.3), Day 2.

On Day 2, the price went down and penetrated the B$_1$ target; however, we do not

Fig. 7.3

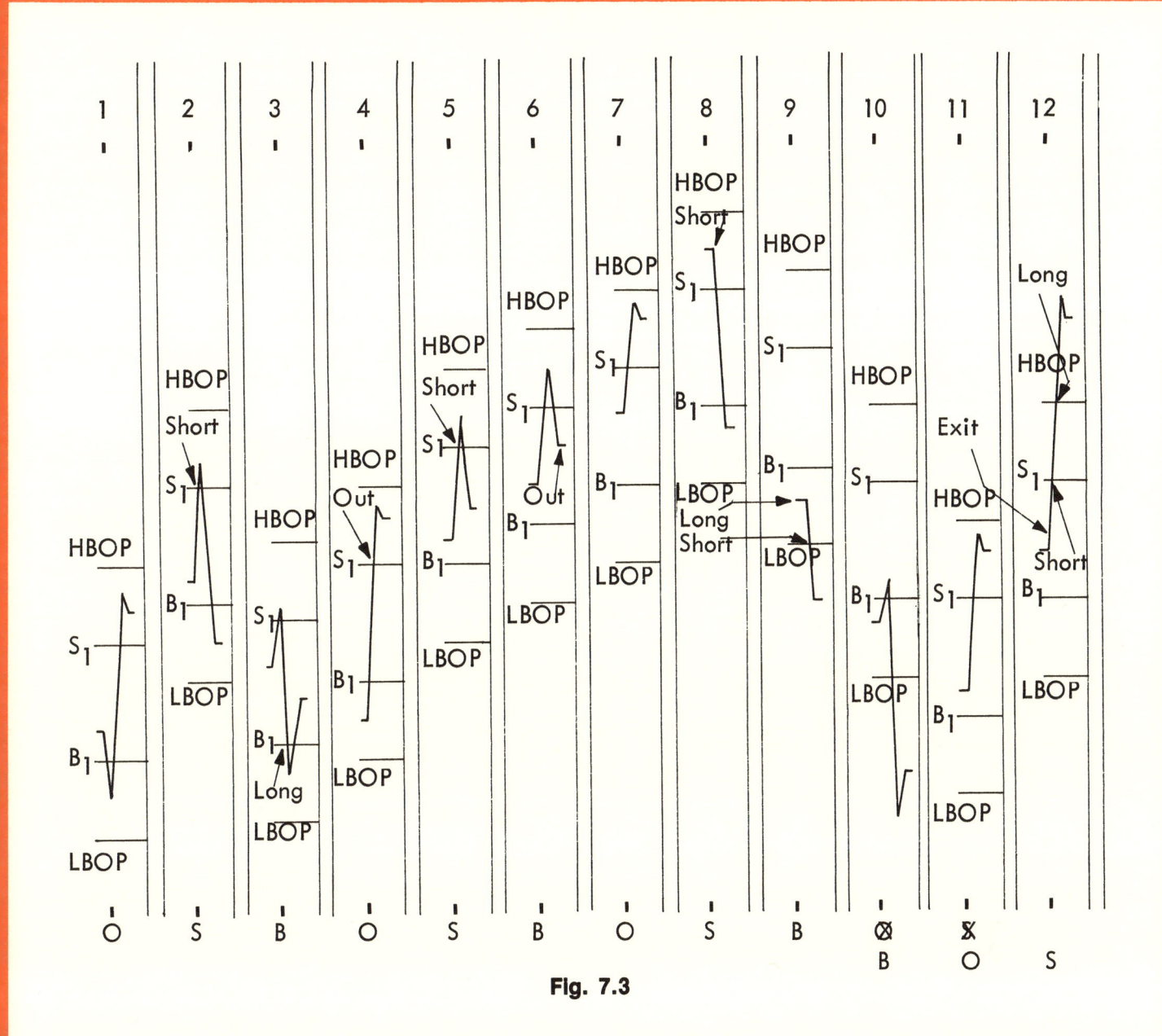

take profits on day of entry. We must wait for the following "B" day to take profits and reverse at B₁.

On Day 3, a "B" day, the price came down, touched the B₁ buy point and we reversed to *Long* because we can only buy on a "B" day.

On Day 4, the price continued up, went through the S₁ point and we took profits at S₁ because **S₁ is a target only on an "O" day.** We cannot reverse and/or initiate a new position on an "O" day while in the Reaction Mode.

On Day 5, an "S" day, we go *Short* at S₁.

On Day 6, a "B" day, the B₁ price is not touched; therefore we exit the market on the **close** of Day 6.

On Day 7, an "O" day, we cannot initiate a new position unless the price penetrates one of the breakout points; in which case, we **would** initiate a position, enacting the Trend Mode and using the trailing stop. This did not occur; therefore, we continue in the Reaction Mode.

On Day 8, an "S" day, the price opened **above** the S₁ point, so we went *Short* on the open. The price then went directly down through the B₁ point and closed on the low. Since we do not exit a trade on the day it is initiated (unless the price penetrates one of the breakout points), we remain in the trade on Day 8.

74

On Day 9, the price opens **below** B_1; therefore, we went *Long* on the open, reversing the previous *Short* position. The price continues to drop, goes through the LBOP and we go *Short*. We are now in Trend Mode and will follow this *Short* trade with the trailing stop.

On the day of the breakout, we use the highest high of the two previous days as the trailing stop. After the market closes, we compare the high made today and the high made yesterday. The higher of the two will be the trailing stop to use for tomorrow.

On Day 10 and Day 11, we remain in the *Short* trade. The trailing stop was not touched.

On Day 12, the price reacts and we exit the market at the trailing stop (which was the high made on Day 11). We **do not reverse**. We are now back in the Reaction Mode (Anti-trend).

PHASING TECHNIQUE

(For use **only after** a Trend Mode Trade)

Now we come to a very important part of this system which has not yet been explained. This part is the PHASING TECHNIQUE, and here is the rule:

(1) The day on which the **lowest** price was reached while in a *Short* TREND MODE trade (initiated by LBOP) is designated as a "B" day; or

(2) The day on which the **highest** price was reached while in a *Long* TREND MODE trade (initiated by HBOP) is designated as an "S" day.

Notice that the lowest price reached while in the *Short* Trend Mode trade was made on Day 10; therefore, Day 10 (which was previously an "O" day) is redesignated as a "B" day. Maintaining the same sequence, Day 11 is then designated as an "O" day, etc.

Here is another important point. Suppose on Day 11 the price had continued to go up and had broken through the HBOP. In this case, we would have gone *Long* at the HBOP which would have put us in the Trend Mode. Our trailing stop for Day 11 would have been the low on Day 10. **It is therefore possible to go from the *Short* Trend Mode to the *Long* Trend Mode and vice versa without initiating a trade in the Reaction Mode.**

Day 12 is an "S" day. We go *Short* at S_1; however, the price continued to go against our position and broke through the HBOP. We reversed and went *Long* at the HBOP. We are now back in Trend Mode and following the price **up** with the trailing stop.

Let's say that the price continues to go up for two more days, reacts, and we exit the market at the trailing stop. We are now back in the Reaction Mode. We must, at this point, ascertain that our phasing is correct. The day upon which the highest price was reached will be an "S" day. If it happens to be an "S" day under the previous phasing, then no change is made; however, if it is **not** an "S" day under the previous phasing, then it must be designated as an "S" day and the phasing continued in the sequence "B", "O", "S", "B", "O", "S", etc.

One other important thing. Can a Reaction Mode trade be initiated on the same day that a Trend Mode is stopped out? The answer is YES . . . if there is at least one day between the lowest or highest day, and the day the Reaction Mode trade is initiated.

If we are stopped out of a *Short* Trend Mode trade, the lowest day will be a "B" day and the following day must be an "O" day, which means that a Reaction Mode trade cannot be initiated until the following "S" day. Conversely, if we are stopped out of a *Long* Trend Mode trade, the highest day will be an "S" day and the following day will be a "B" day. However, **no position can be taken on the "B" day because it cannot be ascertained until the close** that the previous day was, in fact, the highest day.

Now that we have a basic understanding of the system, we will set out the complete rules. Study these rules in light of the previous discussion and then we will recap the procedure, cover the mathematics and work through an example on the work sheet.

REACTION TREND RULES

GENERAL:

Begin trading in REACTION MODE. Switch to TREND MODE on any day that the price crosses a breakout point, HBOP or LBOP. Stay in TREND MODE until stopped out at the trailing stop. **Do not reverse** at the trailing stop. Adjust PHASING if necessary and resume trading in the REACTION MODE.

REACTION MODE:

PHASING:

(1) Find a **significant low point** two to three weeks prior to initiating the first trade. Designate the day of this low point as a "B" day. Designate all following days in sequence, "O", "S", "B", "O", "S", etc.

(2) If a previous high point is most significant, then designate that day as an "S" day and continue the sequence "B", "O", "S", etc. The initial phasing may also be determined by the following Rule (3).

(3) Whenever the price penetrates a breakout point, HBOP or LBOP, adjust, if necessary, the phasing as follows:

   (A) Designate the **highest** day while in a *Long* TREND MODE trade as an "S" day and continue the sequence, "B", "O", "S", etc.

   (B) Designate the **lowest** day while in a *Short* TREND MODE trade as a "B" day and continue the sequence, "O", "S", "B", etc.

ENTRY:

(1) *Long* at B_1 on a "B" day **only**.

(2) *Short* at S_1 on an "S" day **only**.

EXIT: (non-reversing)

(1) From a *Long* position:
   (A) At S_1 on an "O" day.
   (B) At CLOSE on an "S" day if S_1 (reverse point) is not touched.
   (C) Do not exit on day of entry except at LBOP which is a **reverse** on **any** day.

(2) From a *Short* position:
   (A) At CLOSE on a "B" day if B_1 (reverse point) is not touched.
   (B) Do not exit on day of entry except at HBOP which is a **reverse** on **any** day.

REVERSE:

(1) From a *Long* position:
    (A) At S1 on an "S" day.
    (B) At LBOP on any day.

(2) From a *Short* position:
    (A) At B1 on a "B" day.
    (B) At HBOP on any day.

TREND MODE

ENTRY:

(1) *Long* at HBOP on any day.
(2) *Short* at LBOP on any day.

EXIT:

(1) From a *Long* position at the trailing stop. (The lower of the two previous day's lows.) This is a stop only — not a reverse.
(2) From a *Short* position at the trailing stop. (The higher of the two previous day's highs.) This is a stop only — not a reverse.

REVERSE:

None in Trend Mode.

Before we explain the mathematics for this system, let's review the options we have for each day:

On the "B" day, let's assume we went *Long* at B_1. On this day, we do not exit at the S_1 price action point. We will exit on the "B" day **only** if the price goes against us enough to cross the LBOP, at which point we will reverse to *Short*. Let's say that the price moved in our favor on the "B" day. When the market closes, we take the high, low and close price and generate the price action points for the following day, which is an "O" day.

On the "O" day, we have two options. If the price moves far enough in our favor to touch S_1 we will take our profits and get out of the market — we will **not** reverse. If the price goes through a breakout point, we will enter the Trend Mode and follow the price with the trailing stop. If the price does not reach S_1 on the "O" day nor does it go through a breakout point, then no action is taken on the "O" day. When the market closes, we calculate the price action points for the following "S" day.

On the "S" day, we **must** exit the *Long* position one way or another. On the "S" day, there are three options available to us. If the price continues to go in our favor and touches the S_1 sell point, we will **reverse** our position at that point. If the price crosses a breakout point, we will follow the Trend Mode. If the price does neither of these, we will **exit on the close**, but **will not reverse**. In this case, we will plan to go *Long* the following "B" day at B_1. (If the price does **not** go down enough on the "B" day to trigger B_1, we will stay out of the market.)

Now let's say that on the "S" day we are reversed at S_1. As soon as we are reversed, our stop is the HBOP which is a reverse to put us *Long* in the Trend Mode. If the price drops down and crosses B_1 on the "S" day, we **do not exit** but stay with the position. Let's say that when the market closes on the "S" day, we are still *Short*. We calculate the price action points for the following "B" day.

On the "B" day we **must** exit the *Short* position one way or the other. If, on the "B" day, the price goes down and touches B_1, we will reverse from *Short* to *Long*. If this happens, the stop will be the LBOP which is also a reverse to put us in the Trend Mode with a *Short* position. However, if the price on the "B" day **does not** go low enough to reverse our open *Short* position at B_1 and **does not** go high enough to reverse into the Trend Mode at HBOP, then we will exit the market on the **close**. If this happens, we could not take a new position on the following "O" day but would wait and try to take a *Short* position on the "S" day at S_1. If the price never reaches S_1 on the "S" day, we will still be out of the market and would attempt to enter *Long* at B_1 on the following "B" day.

On **any** day that the price crosses either the HBOP or the LBOP, we are automatically in Trend Mode and follow **only the Trend Mode rules** until stopped out by the trailing stop.

Normally, we would enter Trend Mode on a reversal or new entry from the Reaction Mode trade; however, it is possible, if we are **not** in the market while the system is in Reaction Mode, that the price could **open above** the HBOP or **below** the LBOP. In this case, we would enter either *Long* or *Short* as applicable. This is the only way we could enter the Trend Mode without reversing from the Reaction Mode if we were not in an open position.

Now let's look at a hypothetical example illustrated on the following chart and work sheet.

The prices for Day 1 are as follows:

High: 51.50   Low: 50.50   Close: 50.50

The prices for Day 1 are used to calculate the price action points for Day 2.

DAILY WORK SHEET

THE REACTION TREND SYSTEM

DATE		OPEN	HIGH	LOW	CLOSE	$\bar{X}$	$2\bar{X}-H$ B_1	$2\bar{X}-L$ S_1	$2\bar{X}-2L+H$ HBOP	$2\bar{X}-2H+L$ LBOP
1	S	51.00	51.50	50.50	50.50					
2	B	50.50	51.00	50.00	51.00	50.83	50.16	51.16	52.16	49.16
3	O	51.00	51.20	50.50	51.00	50.67	50.34	51.34	52.34	49.34
4	S	51.10	51.50	50.50	50.50	50.90	50.60	51.30	52.00	49.90
5	B	51.00	51.00	50.10	51.00	50.83	50.16	51.16	52.16	49.16
6	O	50.50	50.50	49.00	49.50	50.70	50.40	51.30	52.20	49.50
7	S	49.50	49.50	48.00	48.00	49.67	48.84	50.34	51.84	47.34
8	B	48.00	48.50	47.50	47.80	48.50	47.50	49.00	50.50	46.00
9	OB	47.20	48.20	47.00	48.20	47.93	47.36	48.36	49.36	46.36
10	O	48.50	49.50	47.70	49.50	47.80	47.40	48.60	49.80	46.20
11	S	49.80	50.50	49.00	49.20	48.90	48.30	50.10	51.90	46.50
12	B	49.00	49.75	48.80	49.40	49.57	48.64	50.14	51.64	47.14
13	O	49.50	50.30	49.30	50.30	49.32	48.89	49.84	50.79	47.94
14	S	50.00	50.80	49.60	49.80	49.97	49.64	50.64	51.64	48.64
15	B	49.80	50.50	49.20	50.20	50.07	49.34	50.54	51.74	48.14
16	O	50.00	50.20	49.50	50.10	49.97	49.44	50.74	52.04	48.14
17	S	49.80	49.80	48.90	48.90	49.93	49.66	50.36	51.06	48.96
18	B	49.00	49.50	48.50	49.20	49.20	48.60	49.50	50.40	47.70
19	O	49.50	49.80	49.00	49.20	49.07	48.64	49.64	50.64	47.64
20	S	49.00	49.70	48.80	49.30	49.33	48.86	49.66	50.46	48.06
21	B	49.40	49.85	49.00	49.20	49.27	48.84	49.74	50.64	47.94
						49.35	48.85	49.70	50.55	48.00
22	O	49.50	50.00	49.00	49.50					
23	S	49.50	50.00	49.00	49.50	49.50	49.00	50.00	51.00	48.00
24	B	49.50	50.00	49.00	49.50	49.50	49.00	50.00	51.00	48.00
25	O	49.50	50.00	49.00	49.50	49.50	49.00	50.00	51.00	48.00
26	S	49.50	50.00	49.00	49.50	49.50	49.00	50.00	51.00	48.00
27	B	49.50	50.00	49.00	49.50	49.50	49.00	50.00	51.00	48.00
28	O	49.50	50.00	49.00	49.50	49.50	49.00	50.00	51.00	48.00
						49.50	49.00	50.00	51.00	48.00

COMMODITY _____ CONTRACT MONTH _____

ENTRY	EXIT	P&L	ACTION and ORDER
50.16			Accum
51.30	51.30	+1.14	
50.16	50.16	+1.14	+2.28
49.50	49.50	-.66	+1.62
	48.50	+1.00	+2.62
50.10			
	49.40	+.50	+3.12
50.64			
49.34	49.34	+1.30	+4.42
	48.90	-.44	+3.98
48.60			
	49.64	+1.04	+5.02
49.66			
	49.20	+.46	+5.48
50.00			
49.00	49.00	+1.00	
	50.00	+1.00	
50.00			
49.00	49.00	+1.00	
	50.00	+1.00	

80

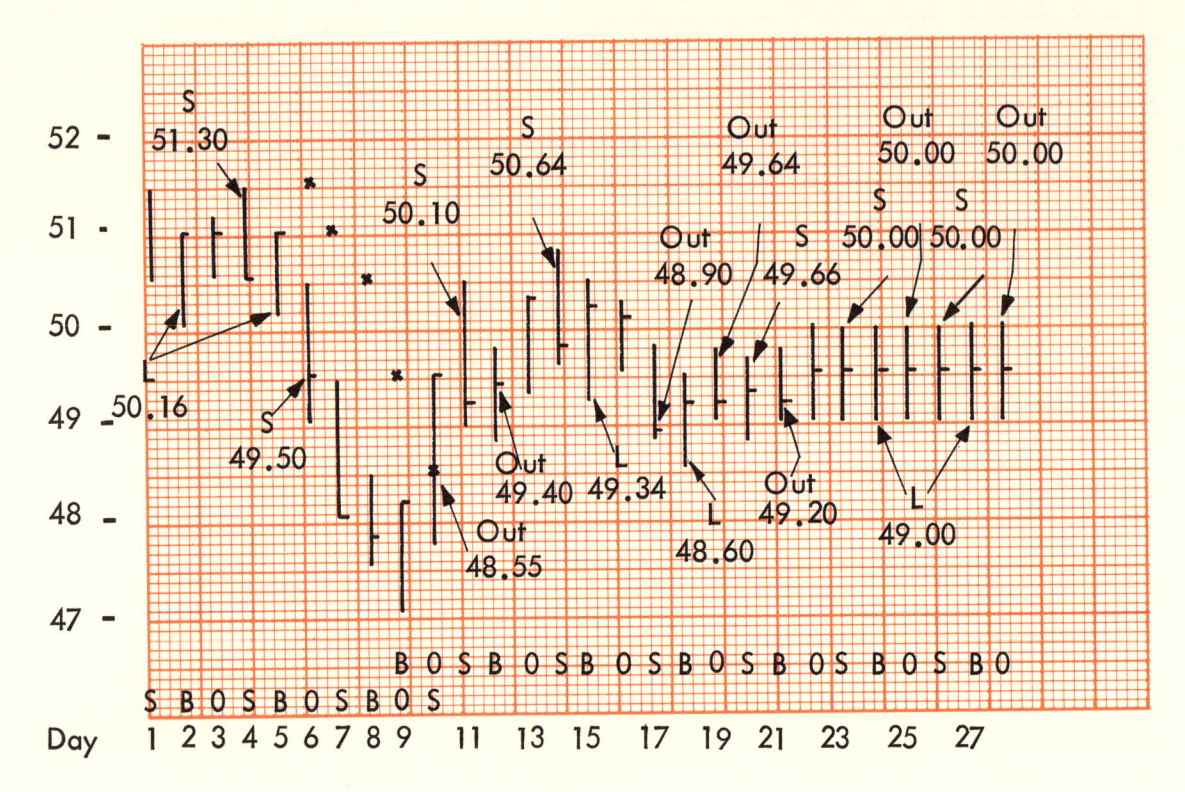

Fig. 7.4

$$\overline{X} = \frac{H + L + C}{3}$$

$$= \frac{51.50 + 50.50 + 50.50}{3}$$

$$= \frac{152.50}{3} = 50.83$$

(1) B_1 = 2 $\overline{X}$ — H
          = 2 (50.83) — 51.50
          = 101.66 — 51.50 = 50.16

(2) S_1 = 2 $\overline{X}$ — L
          = 2 (50.83) — 50.50
          = 101.66 — 50.50 = 51.16

(3)   HBOP = 2 $\overline{X}$ — 2 L + H
              = 2 (50.83) — 2 (50.50) + 51.50
              = 101.66 — 101.00 + 51.50
              = 52.16

(4)   LBOP = 2 $\overline{X}$ — 2 H + L
              = 2 (50.83) — 2 (51.50) + 50.50
              = 101.66 — 103.00 + 50.50
              = 49.16

NEW CONCEPTS IN TECHNICAL TRADING SYSTEMS

Now that we have calculated the four price action points for Day 2, we insert them in the appropriate columns on the line for Day 2. For this example, we will assume we have determined that Day 1 is an "S" day and therefore, Day 2 is a "B" day.

Since Day 2 is a "B" day, we are concerned with only three of the four price action points; i.e., B_1, LBOP, and HBOP. On the following "B" day, we will attempt to go *Long* at 50.16. The stop and reverse is the LBOP at 49.16

On Day 2, the price touches B_1 and we go *Long* in the market at 50.16. After the market closes this day, we calculate the four price action points for Day 3, which is an "O" day. On the "O" day, we will attempt to exit the market at S_1 if reached.

On Day 3, the high was 51.20 so we did not reach the S_1 target of 51.34. We calculate the four price action points for Day 4 and note that the S_1 for Day 4 is 51.30.

On Day 4, the price hit S_1 and we reversed our position to *Short* at 51.30. We also gave the broker our stop and reverse point, the HBOP at 52.00.

Day 5 is a "B" day and we reverse the *Short* position to *Long* at B_1, 50.16. The stop and reverse point after taking the *Long* position is the LBOP at 49.16.

On Day 6, the price falls out of bed and dives through the LBOP at 49.50. We go *Short* at this point and are now in Trend Mode. We immediately give the broker the stop for today of 51.50, which is the higher high of the two previous days.

Our trailing stop for Day 7 is 51.00.

On Day 8, the trailing stop is 50.50. On Day 9, the trailing stop is 49.50. On Day 10, we are stopped out at the trailing stop at 48.50. Since this is a Trend Mode trade, we do not reverse but simply exit the market at the stop. The first thing we must do after being stopped out of a Trend Mode trade is to check the phasing to see if it needs to be adjusted. The lowest day while in the Trend Mode trade was Day 9, which was an "O" day according to the original phasing. After the market closed on Day 10, we can recognize Day 9 as being the **lowest** day while in the *Short* Trend Mode trade. We therefore designate Day 9 as a "B" day, Day 10 as an "O" day, and Day 11 as an "S" day, etc.

Having just exited the Trend Mode, we are automatically back in Reaction Mode. Day 10 is an "O" day; therefore, we initiate no trades on the "O" day unless, of course, the price penetrates the HBOP or LBOP.

On Day 11, the price hits S_1 at 50.10 and we go *Short* at this price.

Day 12 is a "B" day and we want to cover the *Short* position at B_1, which is 48.64. However, the price does not get that low, so we exit the market on the close that day. We do not take a *Long* position unless the B_1 price is touched.

Day 13 is an "O" day and since we are not in the market, we must remain neutral until the following "S" day unless the price goes through the HBOP or LBOP.

On Day 14, we go *Short* at S_1 at 50.64.

On Day 15, the following "B" day, we reverse our *Short* position at B_1 and go *Long* at 49.34.

Day 16 is an "O" day and we hold our position because the S_1 target was not reached. (Notice that S_1 for Day 17, the "S" day, is lower than for Day 16. This is because the move on Day 16 did not carry through and therefore produced a lower target for Day 17.)

The price on Day 17 still did not hit the reduced target, so we exited on the close that day.

On Day 18, a "B" day, the price touches B_1 and we go *Long*.

On Day 19, the following "O" day, the S_1 target of 49.64 is reached and we exit the market at that point. We do not reverse.

On Day 20, we go *Short* at S_1 at 49.66.

On Day 21, the B_1 of 48.84 is not reached, so we exit the *Short* position on the close at 49.20. Notice that this system often produces a profit even when the B_1 or S_1 points are not reached.

Day 22 is an "O" day, so no new positions are initiated since the price did not cross the HBOP or LBOP.

Now, just for fun, let's see what happens when we have an absolute sideways market; that is, the high, low and close price for each day is identical. Since Day 22 is an "O" day, the first position we can take is on Day 23.

We go *Short* at S_1 at 50.00. The following day, we reverse at B_1 at 49.00. On Day 25, an "O" day, we take our profits at 50.00 and are out of the market. On Day 26, an "S" day, we go *Short* at 50.00. On Day 27, we go *Long* at B_1, 49.00. On Day 28, an "O" day, we exit the market at 50.00, which is S_1. This hypothetical example shows the inherent characteristics of this system which enable it to be profitable in a very low directional non-trending type of market. Often this type of market is the "lull before the storm," that is, it precedes a dramatic breakout one way or the other. If you are **in** the market with the system when the breakout does occur, there is no way you can miss it.

For simplicity in the preceding example, we entered the market at the breakout price and exited at the trailing stop price. However, when trading this system in the actual market, always **increase** the distance of these points by several ticks. These points are:

(1) HBOP
(2) LBOP
(3) TRAILING STOP

Even though it may take several readings, I hope this System has been presented so it is understandable to the reader.

Following is a chart of May 1977 Soybean Meal which shows the system trading in this type of market. I think you will agree that this system is worth the effort it may take to master it.

Reaction Trend System — May 1977 Soybean Meal

Chart No.	BOS Sequence	Position	Price	Entry/Exit Signal	P & L	Accum
1	O	L	159.00*	HBOP		
2	B	Out	162.70*	T-stop	+ 3.70	
3	O	L	167.90*	HBOP		
4	O/B	Out	194.80	T-Stop	+26.90	+30.60
5	S	S	191.10	LBOP		
6	S	Out	204.00*	T-Stop	—12.90	+17.70
7	B	S	192.10	LBOP		
8	S	Out	201.00*	T-Stop	— 8.90	+ 8.80
9	S	S	204.00	S_1		
10	S	L	208.20	HBOP	— 4.20	+ 4.60
11	S/B	Out	223.50	T-Stop	+15.30	+19.90
12	S	S	214.80	LBOP		
13	S/O	Out	197.20	T-Stop	+17.60	+37.50
14	B	L	192.30	B_1		
15	B	S	188.10	LBOP	— 4.20	+33.30
16	O/S	Out	185.70	T-Stop	+ 2.40	+35.70
17	B	L	184.00	B_1		
18	O	Out	187.30	S_1	+ 3.30	+39.00
19	B	L	183.60	B_1		
20	O	Out	184.70	S_1	+ 1.10	+40.10
21	O	L	185.90	HBOP		
22	O	Out	188.80	T-Stop	+ 2.90	+43.00
23	S	S	188.30	S_1		
24	B	Out/L	194.50*	B_1/HBOP	— 6.20	+36.80
25	O/B	Out	194.00*	T-Stop	+ .50	+37.30
26	S	S	199.00	S_1		
27	B	L	195.30	B_1	+ 3.70	+41.00
28	S	Out	195.00**		+ .30	+41.30
29	B	L	198.90	HBOP		
30	S/B	Out	207.30	T-Stop	+ 8.40	+49.70
31	S	S	198.80	LBOP		
32	S/B	Out	184.20	T-Stop	+14.70	+64.30
33	S	S	190.70	S_1		
34	B	B	192.00	B_1	— 1.30	+63.00
35	O	S	189.20	LBOP		
36	O/S	Out	192.50*	T-Stop	— 3.30	+59.70
37	B	S	190.00	LBOP		
38	O/S	Out	183.90	T-Stop	+ 6.10	+65.80
39	O	L	189.90	HBOP		
40	O	Out	188.80	T-Stop	— 1.10	+64.70
41	B	L	189.00	B_1		
42	S	Out/S	190.50	S_1	+ 1.50	+66.20
43	O	Out	191.70	T-Stop	— 1.20	+65.00
44	S	S	182.50*	LBOP		
45	S	Out	182.70	T-Stop	— .20	+64.80
46	S	S	188.60	S_1		
47	B	Out/L	193.20	HBOP	— 4.60	+60.20

Chart No.	BOS Sequence	Position	Price	Entry/Exit Signal	P & L	Accum
48	O/S	Out	192.30	T-Stop	— .90	+59.30
49	B	L	190.60	B_1		
50	O	Out	194.10	S_1	+ 3.50	+62.80
51	B	L	193.30	B_1		
52	O	Out	195.50*	S_1	+ 2.20	+65.00
53	O	L	198.00	HBOP		
54	O	Out	200.00*	T-Stop	+ 2.00	+67.00
55	S	S	200.20	S_1		
56	S	L	202.40	HBOP	— 2.20	+64.80
57	B/S	Out	197.80	T-Stop	— 4.60	+60.20
58	S	S	199.30	S_1		
59	B	Out/L	198.50	B_1	+ .80	+61.00
60	O	Out	200.80	S_1	+ 2.30	+63.30
61	S	S	200.50	S_1		
62	B	Out	204.20**		— 3.70	+59.60
63	S	S	207.40	S_1		
64	B	Out/L	205.30	B_1	+ 2.10	+61.70
65	O	Out	209.40	S_1	+ 4.10	+65.80
66	S	S	213.40	S_1		
67	B	Out	215.30**		— 1.90	+63.90
68	S	S	215.50	S_1		
69	S	L	217.70	HBOP	— 2.20	+61.70
70	O	Out	213.30	T-Stop	— 4.40	+57.30
71	S	S	215.00	S_1		
72	B	Out/L	214.00	B_1	+ 1.00	+58.30
73	S	Out/S	217.30	S_1	+ 3.30	+61.60
74	B	L	212.30	B_1	+ 5.00	+66.60
75	O	Out	213.00	S_1	+ .70	+67.30
76	O	L	215.90	HBOP		
77	B/O	Out	210.00	T-Stop	— 5.90	+61.40
78	S	S	214.30	S_1		
79	B	Out/L	208.90	B_1	+ 5.40	+66.80
80	S	Out	210.70**		+ 1.80	+68.40
81	B	L	209.10	B_1		
82	O	Out	209.60	S_1	+ .50	+69.10
83	S	S	210.80	S_1		
84	B	Out	212.40**		— 1.60	+67.50
85	S	S	214.80	S_1		
86	B	Out	213.20**		+ 1.60	+69.10
87	B	L	211.20	B_1		
88	O	Out	211.30	S_1	+ .10	+69.20
89	O	L	213.00	HBOP		
90	S	Out	236.30	T-Stop	+23.30	+92.50
91	S	S	234.20	S_1		
92	B	L	234.00	B_1	+ .20	+92.70
93	S	S	238.60	S_1	+ 4.60	+97.30
94	B	L	237.50	B_1	+ 1.00	+98.30
95	O	Out	238.50	S_1	+ .90	+99.20

* Open
** Close

Recap: Reaction Trend System
    (May 77 Soybean Meal)

Trades: 36 profit (64%)
            20 loss (36%)
            56 total

Profits: 174.70 points profit
           75.50 points loss
           99.20 points total profit

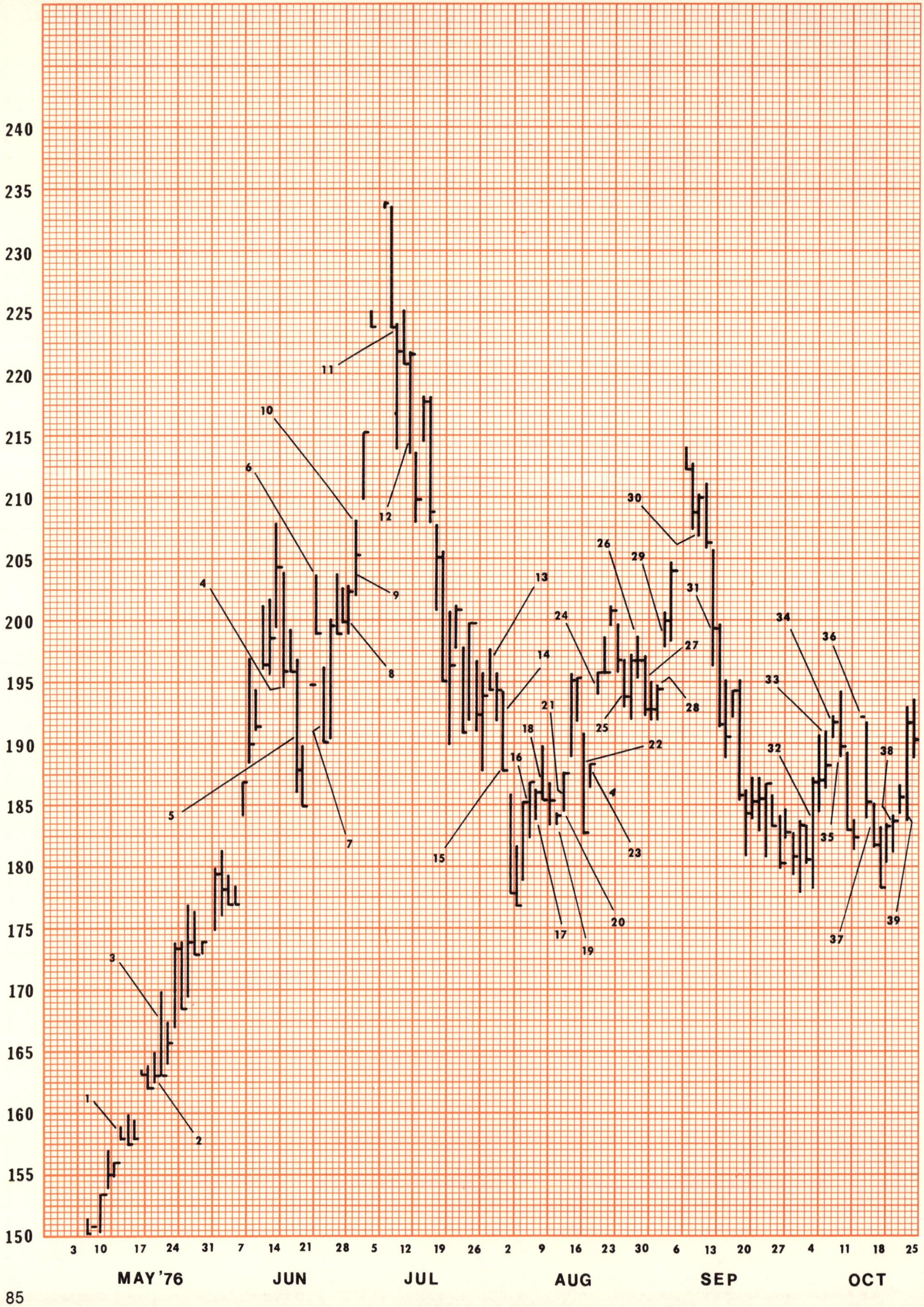

240
235
230
225
220
215
210
205
200
195
190
185
180
175
170
165
160
155
150
3 10 17 24 31 7 14 21 28 5 12 19 26 2 9 16 23 30 6 13 20 27 4 11 18 25
MAY '76
JUN
JUL
AUG
SEP
OCT
1 2 3 4 5 6 7 8 9 10 11 12 13 14 15 16 17 18 19 20 21 22 23 24 25 26 27 28 29 30 31 32 33 34 35 36 37 38 39

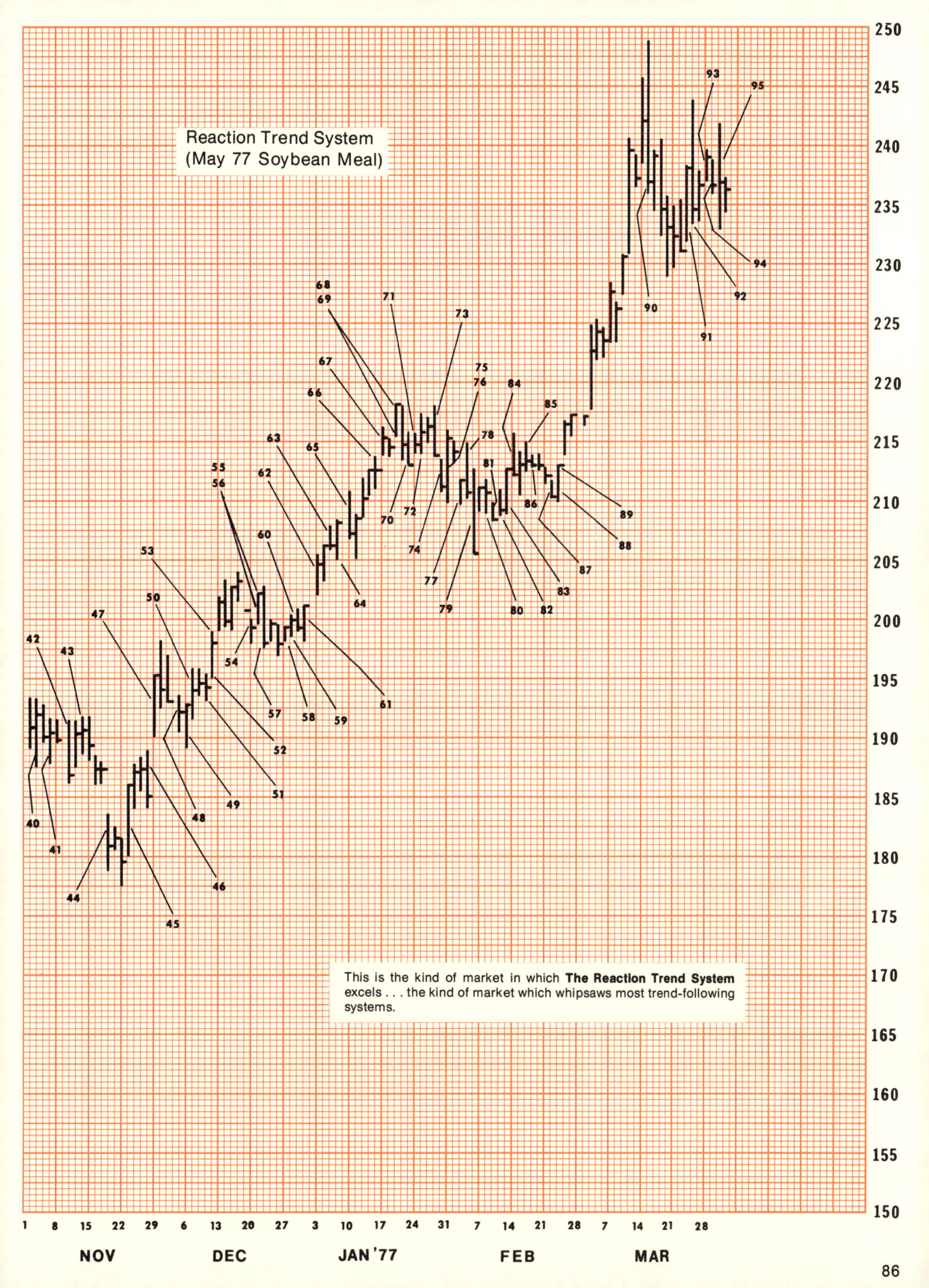

**Reaction Trend System
(May 77 Soybean Meal)**

This is the kind of market in which **The Reaction Trend System** excels... the kind of market which whipsaws most trend-following systems.

86

SECTION VIII

THE SWING INDEX

One of the smartest technicians I know put me on the trail of this method with the following statement:

"Somewhere amidst the maze of Open, High, Low and Close prices is a phantom line that is the REAL market. This line is also indicative of the REAL swings the market is making."

After some study, I concluded that if each day's action could be evaluated definitively, within constant parameters, the phantom line could be revealed. The problem was to compare each day's action within the day and with that of the previous day and relate this action to an absolute.

The problem is compounded by the fact that there are no less than 28 points of evaluation within a two day period. The 16 following points can be compared **between the two days.** The subscript "1" is for the first day, the subscript "2" is for the second day:

H_2H_1	H_2L_1	L_2O_1	O_2C_1
L_2L_1	H_2O_1	L_2C_1	C_2H_1
O_2O_1	H_2C_1	O_2H_1	C_2L_1
C_2C_1	L_2H_1	O_2L_1	C_2O_1

The following six points can be compared **within each day:**

H_1O_1	L_1O_1	H_2O_2	L_2O_2
H_1L_1	L_1C_1	H_2L_2	L_2C_2
H_1C_1	O_1C_1	H_2C_2	O_2C_2

After devising and testing innumerable approaches, the following factors were isolated as the most indicative:

For an UP day, the most indicative PLUS factors are as follows:

(1) Close today above previous close.
(2) Close today above open today.
(3) High today above previous close.
(4) Low today above previous close.
(5) Previous close above previous open.

For a DOWN day, these same factors would have a MINUS value.

These factors were then weighted and evaluated relative to the highest or lowest possible value and defined on a scale with absolute limits.

(1) The highest value for a day would be LIMIT UP from a LIMIT UP day.

(2) The lowest value for a day would be LIMIT DOWN from a LIMIT DOWN day.

(3) A zero value would be a NO CHANGE day from a NO CHANGE day.

(4) The absolute limits would be +100 and —100.

The following equation was derived to satisfy these prerequisites:

$$SI = 50 \left[\frac{C_2 - C_1 + .5(C_2 - O_2) + .25(C_1 - O_1)}{R} \right] \frac{K}{L}$$

Now, before we take up the mathematics for this equation, let's look at how the equation evaluates certain plus and minus factors relative to two day's action. Assume the value of a LIMIT move is 3.00.

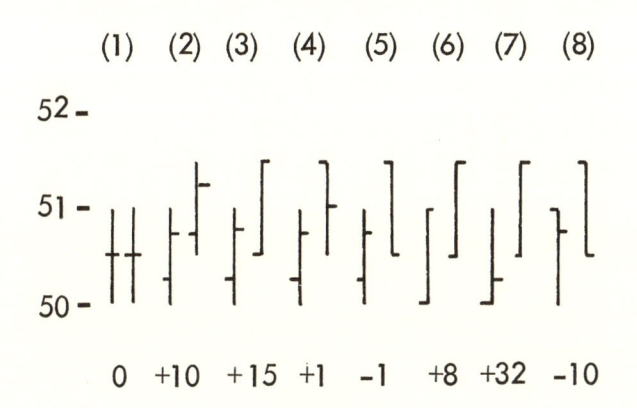

```
      (1)  (2)  (3)  (4)  (5)  (6)  (7)  (8)
52 -
51 -
50 -
       0  +10  +15  +1   -1   +8  +32  -10
```
Fig. 8.1

```
       (9) (10) (11) (12) (13) (14) (15)
54 -
53 -
52 -
51 -
50 -
      +14 +26 +40 +72 +85 +96 +100
```
Fig. 8.2

At first glance, the above values may seem contradictory. The highs and lows for every two days are the same, yet the value for the days varies from —10 to +32. However, when each example is evaluated in light of the five PLUS factors as set out previously, then the values fall into place. Example 7 had the most weighted PLUS factors and closed UP the highest from the previous day. In examples 5 and 8, the MINUS factors outweighted the plus factors and each also closed DOWN from the previous day. In fact, most technicians would call both of these days "Key Reversal" days because the second day

(1) Opened higher
(2) Had a higher high
(3) Closed lower

than the first day.

Take a few minutes and study these first eight examples in light of the five PLUS factors.

Now let's look at a few more examples. Assume the same 3.00 limit as the maximum allowable move in either direction from the previous day's close.

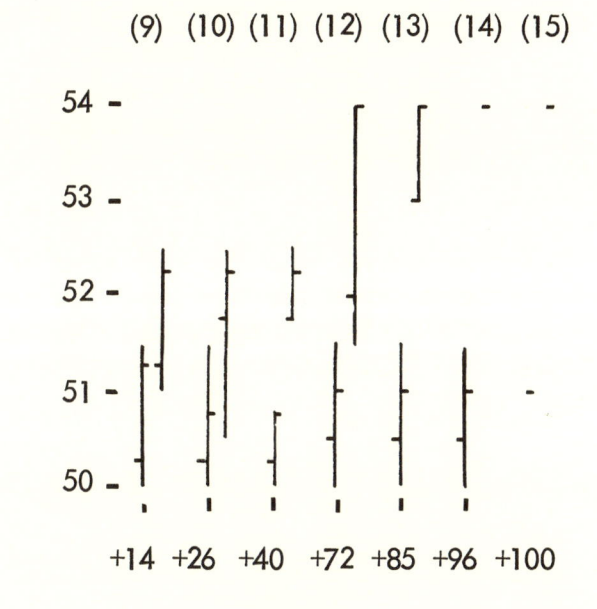

Example 9 The configuration is the same as Example 2; however, the index value is higher because the price moved farther compared to the value of a limit move.

Example 10 The index value is higher than Example 9 because of the higher close compared to the previous day.

Example 11 The opens and closes are identical to Example 10; however, Example 11 has a higher index value because of the GAP caused by the low of Day 2 being **above** the close of Day 1. (In the equation, GAPS are measured between L_2 and C_1, not L_2 and H_1 as is the common practice.)

Example 12 The close for Day 2 is LIMIT UP; yet the index value is 72, not 100.

Example 13 The close for Day 2 here is also LIMIT UP; yet there was trading below the limit. This larger gap indicates a stronger index value than Example 12.

Example 14 Here the price is locked LIMIT for Day 2 and the index value is greater than the previous LIMIT day which had a trading range.

Example 15 Here is LOCKED LIMIT from a LOCKED LIMIT day and the equation gives the highest possible value of 100 because there was no trading range for either day.

Now that we have an insight into the rating characteristics of the equation relative to the index value, let's look at another important feature of the SWING INDEX equation, that of identifying swings:

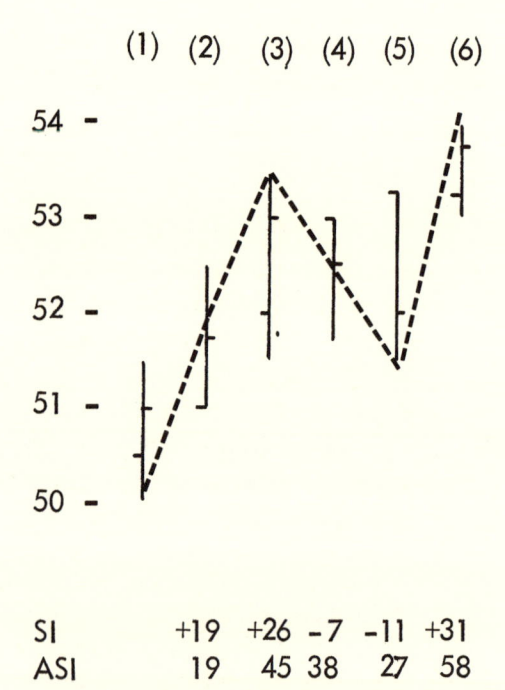

```
              (1)  (2)  (3)  (4)  (5)  (6)
SI                 +19  +26  -7   -11  +31
ASI                 19   45   38   27   58
```

Fig. 8.3

In Fig. 8.3, most technicians would have readily identified the short-term swing as shown. The SWING INDEX also identified the swing, Fig. 8.4. This was done by simply accumulating the index value of each day and graphing the results.

The result is the ACCUMULATIVE SWING INDEX (ASI). It is obtained by adding or subtracting (as indicated by the sign + or —) each day's value from the previous **total** value.

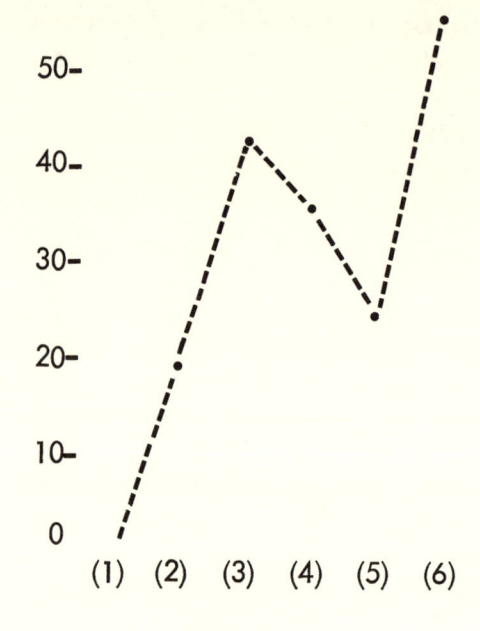

Fig. 8.4

In Fig. 8.4, we start at 0, add to this the value for the second day of +19 and the ASI for Day 2 is +19. On Day 3, the SI is 26. Add this to +19 and the ASI for Day 3 is 45. On Day 4, the SI is —7. Subtract this from 45 and the ASI for Day 4 is 38, etc.

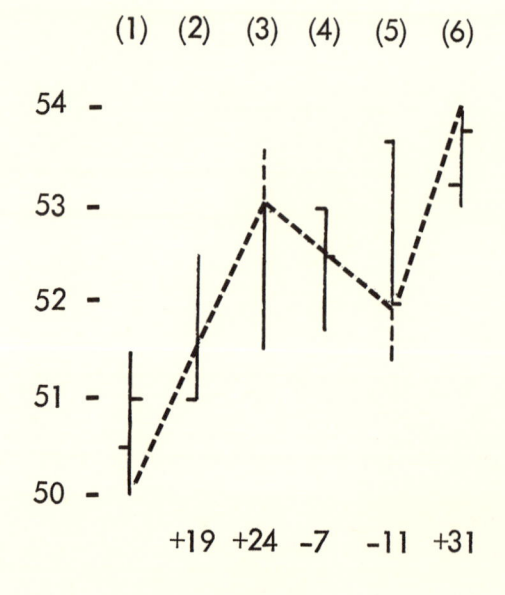

+19 +24 -7   -11 +31

Fig. 8.5

Now look at Fig. 8.5, which is identical to Fig. 8.3 except for the high on Day 3 and the low on Day 5. Most technicians would not have identified this swing; however, by evaluating each day's action, the ASI picks up the swing.

I realize that there are few, if any, definitive rules accepted by every technician for positively identifying swings. In fact, there are probably as many different rules for identifying swings as there are swing systems. Add to these the practitioners of the Elliott Wave Theory and it is obvious that the value of an equation which will identify the short-term swings mathematically without **any rules** is certainly a significant concept.

The implications for being able to plug the four daily prices into an equation which will give a **one number relative value** for the day's trading and also identify precisely all short term swings are far reaching indeed. Those readers who like to use their own creative ability and ingenuity to devise workable systems will have a field day with this concept.

I wanted to take the time to show the reader the value and the results of this equation before explaining it. The reason is that this equation is not overly simple for the non-mathematically inclined; however, solving the equation is only a matter of adding, subtracting, multiplying and dividing.

In the SI equation, use the ABSOLUTE VALUE of all terms **except** those in the numerator inside the brackets. The numerator is all terms on the line above R inside the brackets.

SWING INDEX EQUATION (SI)

$$SI = 50 \left[\frac{C_2 - C_1 + .5(C_2 - O_2) + .25(C_1 - O_1)}{R} \right] \frac{K}{L}$$

Where K = the largest of:

(1) $H_2 - C_1$
(2) $L_2 - C_1$

and L = Value of a limit move in one direction.

To obtain "R", first determine the **largest** of:

(1) $H_2 - C_1$
(2) $L_2 - C_1$
(3) $H_2 - L_2$

If (1) is the largest, $R = (H_2 - C_1) - .5(L_2 - C_1) + .25(C_1 - O_1)$
If (2) is the largest, $R = (L_2 - C_1) - .5(H_2 - C_1) + .25(C_1 - O_1)$
If (3) is the largest, $R = (H_2 - L_2) + .25(C_1 - O_1)$

Where:

O_1 = Yesterday's Open
H_1 = " High
L_1 = " Low
C_1 = " Close

O_2 = Today's Open
H_2 = " High
L_2 = " Low
C_2 = " Close

Now let's work out an example using the following prices:

	Open	High	Low	Close
Day 1	50.50	52.00	50.00	51.50
Day 2	51.80	53.00	51.30	52.80

First we will obtain the numerator: (N)

$$N = C_2 - C_1 + .5(C_2 - O_2) + .25(C_1 - O_1)$$

(Substituting)

$$N = 52.80 - 51.50 + .5(52.80 - 51.80) + .25(51.50 - 50.50)$$
$$= 1.3 + .5(1.00) + .25(.1.00)$$
$$= 1.3 + .50 + .25$$

$$N = 2.05$$

We will put the numerical equivalents in the SI Equation as they are obtained. We will assume the LIMIT (L) is 3.00. So far:

$$SI = 50 \left[\frac{2.05}{} \right] \left[\frac{}{3.00} \right]$$

K = the greater of:

(1) $H_2 - C_1$: substituting $53.00 - 51.50 = 1.50$
or: (2) $L_2 - C_1$: substituting $51.30 - 51.50 = .20$ (ABS)

K therefore is 1.50.

$$SI = 50 \left[\frac{2.05}{} \right] \left[\frac{1.50}{3.00} \right]$$

To obtain R, first determine the **largest** of:

(1) $H_2 - C_1$: substituting $53.00 - 51.50 = 1.50$
(2) $L_2 - C_1$: substituting $51.30 - 51.50 = .20$ (ABS)
(3) $H_2 - L_2$: substituting $53.00 - 51.30 = 1.70$

Since (3) above is the largest, we will find R by substituting in R (3) equation.

$$R = H_2 - L_2 + .25(C_1 - O_1)$$
$$R = 53.00 - 51.30 + .25(51.50 - 50.50)$$
$$R = 1.70 + .25(1.00)$$
$$R = 1.70 + .25$$
$$R = 1.95$$

Now we have all of the terms for the SI equation.

$$SI = 50\left[\frac{N}{R}\right]\left[\frac{K}{L}\right]$$

$$SI = 50\left[\frac{2.05}{1.95}\right]\left[\frac{1.50}{3.00}\right]$$

First divide the numbers inside the brackets

$$SI = 50 \quad [1.05] \quad .50$$

Now multiply the three numbers together:

SI = 50 x 1.05 x .50
SI = 26.25

And round off to the nearest whole number: SI = 26

There are some short cuts that can be taken. For instance, when we determined the value for K we used these same values in addition to $H_2 - L_2$ to determine which of the three equations to use for R. Also the .25 $(C_1 - O_1)$ term in the R equation had already been obtained as one of the terms in the numerator.

Now let's use these short cuts and find the SI for a DOWN day:

	Open	High	Low	Close
Day 1	53.50	54.00	52.00	52.50
Day 2	52.00	52.00	51.00	51.00

First, obtain the numerator: (N)

N = $C_2 - C_1$ + .5 $(C_2 - O_2)$ + .25 $(C_1 - O_1)$

Substituting: 51.00 — 52.50 + .5 (51.00 — 52.00) + .25 (52.50 — 53.50)

```
    =    —1.50       + .5 ( —1.00 )   + .25 ( —1.00 )
    =    —1.50       —      .50       —       .25
N =      —2.25
```

Note the term 51.00 — 52.50 is —1.50. Also, a plus number times a minus number gives a minus number as an answer.

as: +.5 (—1.00) = —.50

So far, our SI Equation is:

$$SI = 50\left[\frac{N}{R}\right]\left[\frac{K}{L}\right]$$

$$SI = 50\left[\frac{-2.25}{}\right]\left[\frac{}{3.00}\right]$$

The numerator is the only term in which we **do not** use absolute values. (Remember from previous chapters, the absolute value of a plus (+) number being subtracted from a minus (—) number is the difference with the sign of the larger number.)

K = the largest of:

(1) $H_2 - C_1$: substituting 52.00 — 52.50 = .50 (ABS)
(2) $L_2 - C_1$: substituting 51.00 — 52.50 = 1.50 (ABS)

K = 1.50 (the largest absolute value)

To find the equation to use for R, first determine the largest of:

(1) $H_2 - C_1$: found above = .50
(2) $L_2 - C_1$: found above = 1.50
(3) $H_2 - L_2$: substituting 52.00 — 51.00 = 1.00

The largest value is in (2) above, so we use the R(2) equation to find R.

$$R = (L_2 - C_1) - .5(H_2 - C_1) + .25(C_1 - O_1)$$

We found in obtaining the numerator that .25 $(C_1 - O_1)$ was —.25. The absolute value is .25 therefor

R =	(51.00 — 52.50)	—	.5	(52.00 — 52.50)	+	.25	
R =	1.50	—	.5	(—.50)	+	.25	
R =	1.50			—.25	+	.25	
R =	1.50						

therefore:

$$SI = 50 \left[\frac{-2.25}{1.50} \right] \left[\frac{1.50}{3.00} \right]$$

$$SI = 50 [-1.50] \quad .50$$

$$SI = -37.50$$

Note that the sign (+ or —) of the SI is determined by the numerator. If the numerator has a —sign, the index will be minus. If the numerator has a +sign, the index will be plus.

Now for the benefit of those who find the mathematics of the equation a bit tedious, let's look at the work sheet with a set of "cook book" instructions which will work this equation. The headings on the work sheet indicate when to use the absolute value ABS (when to drop the minus sign) and when to use the + or — value (when to keep the minus sign). The following is for the second day on the work sheet.

USE ABSOLUTE VALUES

Put $H_2 - C_1$ in Column #1   44.00 — 41.50 = 2.50
Put $L_2 - C_1$ in Column #2   42.00 — 41.50 = .50
Put $H_2 - L_2$ in Column #3   44.00 — 42.00 = 2.00
Put $C_1 - O_1$ in Column #4   41.50 — 40.50 = 1.00

USE +/— VALUES

Put $C_2 - C_1$ in Column #5 $43.00 - 41.50 = 1.50$
Put $C_2 - O_2$ in Column #6 $43.00 - 42.00 = 1.00$
Put $C_1 - O_1$ in Column #7 $41.50 - 40.50 = 1.00$

$$
\begin{aligned}
N &= \text{Col. \#5} + \tfrac{1}{2}(\text{Col. \#6}) + \tfrac{1}{4}(\text{Col. \#7}) \\
&= 1.50 + \tfrac{1}{2}(1.00) + \tfrac{1}{4}(1.00) \\
&= 1.50 + .50 + .25 \\
N &= 2.25
\end{aligned}
$$

Put N in Column #8.

Find the largest number in Column #1 or Column #2.

Put this in Column #9 (2.50).

Find the largest number in Columns #1, #2, or #3

If in #1, $R = \text{Col. \#1} - \tfrac{1}{2}(\text{Column \#2}) + \tfrac{1}{4}(\text{Column \#4})$
If in #2, $R = \text{Col. \#2} - \tfrac{1}{2}(\text{Column \#1}) + \tfrac{1}{4}(\text{Column \#4})$
If in #3, $R = \text{Col. \#3} + \tfrac{1}{4}(\text{Column \#4})$

Since the largest number is in Column #1, we substitute in the R(1) equation.

$$
\begin{aligned}
R &= 2.50 - \tfrac{1}{2}(.50) + \tfrac{1}{4}(1.00) \\
R &= 2.50 - .25 + .25 \\
R &= 2.50
\end{aligned}
$$

Put R in Column #10 (2.50).

Put the LIMIT in Column #11 (3.00).

$$
\begin{aligned}
SI &= 50 \left[\frac{\text{Column 8}}{\text{Column 10}} \right] \left[\frac{\text{Column 9}}{\text{Column 11}} \right] \\
&= 50 \left[\frac{2.25}{2.50} \right] \left[\frac{2.50}{3.00} \right] \\
&= 50 [.90] [.83] \\
&= 50 \times .90 \times .83 \\
&= 37.35
\end{aligned}
$$

Round off to the nearest whole number:

$SI = 37$

Now let's follow the procedure on the work sheet for a DOWN day. Day 2 (today) is the third day on the work sheet; Day 1 (yesterday) is the second day on the work sheet.

USE ABSOLUTE VALUES

Put $H_2 - C_1$ in Column #1 $43.50 - 43.00 = .50$
Put $L_2 - C_1$ in Column #2 $41.50 - 43.00 = 1.50$ (ABS)
Put $H_2 - L_2$ in Column #3 $43.50 - 41.50 = 2.00$
Put $C_1 - O_1$ in Column #4 $43.00 - 42.00 = 1.00$

USE +/− VALUES

Put $C_2 - C_1$ in Column #5 $42.00 - 43.00 = -1.00$
Put $C_2 - O_2$ in Column #6 $42.00 - 42.80 = -.80$
Put $C_1 - O_1$ in Column #7 $43.00 - 42.00 = 1.00$

$$
\begin{aligned}
N &= \text{Col. \#5} + \tfrac{1}{2}(\text{Column \#6}) + \tfrac{1}{4}(\text{Column \#7}) \\
&= -1.00 + \tfrac{1}{2}(-.80) + \tfrac{1}{4}(1.00) \\
&= -1.00 + -.40 + .25 \\
N &= -1.15
\end{aligned}
$$

Put N in Column #8 (−1.15).

Find the largest of Column #1 or Column #2   (1.50).

Put K in Column #9 (1.50).

Use R(3) equation because Column #3 is the largest of Columns #1, #2, or #3.

$$
\begin{aligned}
R &= \text{Column \#3} + \tfrac{1}{4}(\text{Column \#4}) \\
&= 2.00 + \tfrac{1}{4}(1.00) \\
&= 2.00 + .25 \\
R &= 2.25
\end{aligned}
$$

Put R in column #10 (2.25).

Put the LIMIT in Column #11 (in this example, 3.00)

$$
\begin{aligned}
SI &= 50 \left[\frac{\text{Column 8}}{\text{Column 10}} \right] \left[\frac{\text{Column 9}}{\text{Column 11}} \right] \\
&= 50 \left[\frac{-1.15}{2.25} \right] \left[\frac{1.50}{3.00} \right] \\
&= 50 \quad \times \quad -51 \quad \times \quad 50 \\
&= -12.75 \\
&= -13 \quad \text{(rounded off to the nearest whole number)}
\end{aligned}
$$

The ASI is the ACCUMULATIVE SWING INDEX which is obtained by accumulating each day's SI as indicated by the sign (+ or —) of the latest SI. The accumulative index may be either minus or plus. If the long-term trend is **up**, the accumulative index will be a plus. If the long-term trend is **down** the accumulative index will be a minus. If the long-term trend is non-directional, the ASI will fluctuate from plus to minus.

In the work sheet example, the ASI is the same as the SI on the first day. On the second day, the SI of —13 subtracted from the previous ASI of 37 makes the ASI 24 for the second day, etc.

At the top of the work sheet are brief instructions for obtaining the SI and the ASI using only the work sheet with the column headings and the open, high, low and close prices for the day. By using the work sheet in this manner, even the non-mathematically inclined should have little problem in obtaining the SI and ASI for each trading day. It's like "cook book" engineering. Simply fill in the columns, follow the instructions and it all falls into place.

On the work sheet, the columns have been left blank for days 4 through 8 for those who would like to stop at this point and solve the equation for those five days. The correct answers for each day are filled in under the SI and ASI columns. As with all systems and indexes in this book, there is a blank work sheet for this system in the Appendix. This work sheet can be removed and reproduced on a copier for following the markets on a daily basis.

Let's pause for a minute at this point and consider the significance of the SWING INDEX. The SWING INDEX gives us a numerical value for each day's trading which will always fall between 0 and +100 or 0 and —100. Second, the SWING INDEX gives us definitive short-term swing points. Third, the SWING INDEX gives us a line which cuts through the maze of high, low and close prices and indicates the real strength and direction of the market. Many good systems and methods could be devised based on **one** or a **combination** of these indicators. Those who already use a good swing method or wave method can use this index as an additional tool to indicate by simple mathematics the short-term swings without spending a lot of time with the rules trying to figure out whether a swing is a swing or not. The SWING INDEX can also be used supplementary to other methods as a breakout indicator. A breakout is indicated when the value of the ASI **exceeds** the ASI value on the day when a previous significant HIGH SWING POINT was made. A downside breakout would be indicated when the value of the ASI drops **below** the ASI value on a day when a previous significant LOW SWING POINT was made.

When the SWING INDEX is plotted on the same chart as the daily bar chart, trend lines drawn on the ASI can be compared to trend lines drawn on the bar chart. For those who know how to draw meaningful trend lines, the ASI can be a good tool to confirm trend-line breakouts. Often erroneous breaking of trend lines drawn on bar charts will not be confirmed by the trend lines drawn on the ASI. Since the ASI is heavily weighted in favor of the close price, a quick run up or down during a day's trading does not adversely affect the index.

The system I have devised using the ACCUMULATIVE SWING INDEX is a very simple swing system. The swing points are the HIGH SWING POINTS and LOW SWING POINTS as indicated by the ASI.

SWING INDEX SYSTEM

Initially, the market is entered on a breakout. For instance, we would go *LONG* (Fig. 8.6) the next day when the value of the ASI exceeded the value posted on the day of a previous significant HIGH SWING POINT; or go *SHORT* (Fig. 8.7) the next day when the ASI dropped below the ASI on a day that a previous significant LOW SWING POINT was made.

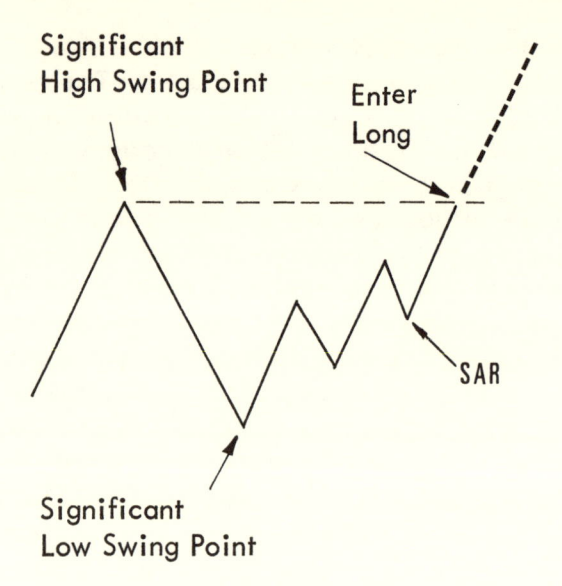

Fig. 8.6

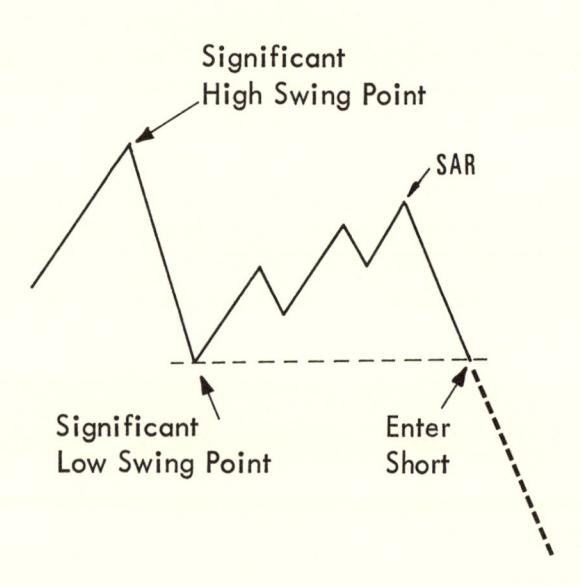

Fig. 8.7

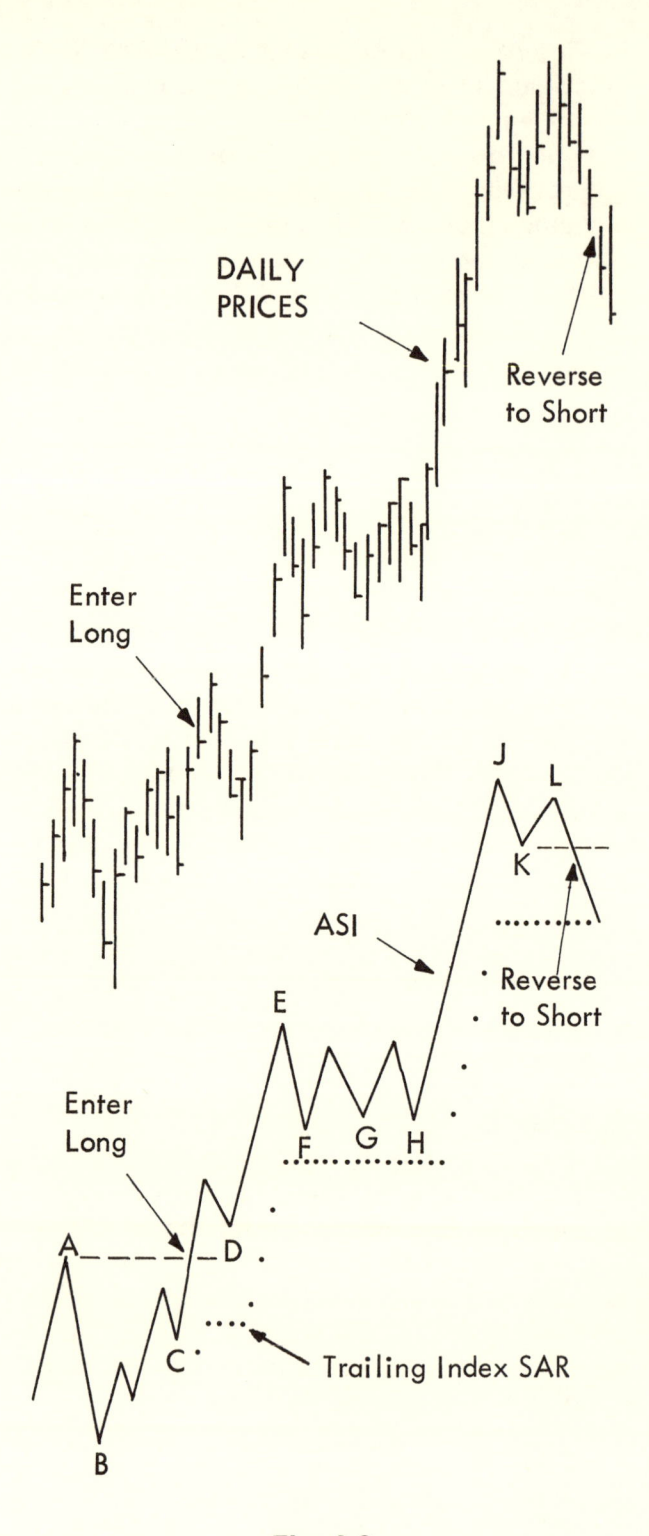

Fig. 8.8

Once in the market, we use the previous swing point as the INDEX STOP AND REVERSE (SAR). If *LONG,* the INDEX SAR is the previous LOW SWING POINT. If *SHORT,* the INDEX SAR is the previous HIGH SWING POINT. In addition, we use an INDEX SAR trailing stop which is 60 points on the ASI from the extreme favorable ASI high (if *LONG)* and from the extreme favorable ASI low (if *SHORT).* This 60 point trailing SAR is 60 points on the ACCUMULATIVE SWING INDEX. The 60 points are **NOT** in terms of the **PRICE** of the commodity being followed.

We go *LONG* initially (Fig. 8.8) when the ASI exceeds the ASI at the significant HIGH SWING POINT (A). The INDEX SAR is point (C) since this is a closer stop than the 60 point trailing INDEX SAR. When point (D) is formed, the INDEX SAR becomes point (D).

97

NEW CONCEPTS IN TECHNICAL TRADING SYSTEMS

There is one more important rule which must be followed in order to cut down the whipsaws when the market stalls; if we are in a *LONG* trade, as in the example, use the **first** LOW SWING POINT after a new HIGH SWING POINT as the INDEX SAR. Then keep the INDEX SAR at this point until the ASI makes a **new high**. After the new high is made, then the **first** LOW SWING POINT formed after the new high becomes the new INDEX SAR.

In Fig. 8.8, after the ASI made a new high at (E), the first LOW SWING POINT was formed at (F). We moved the INDEX SAR to (F) as soon as this point was defined and left it there until the ASI made a new high at point (J) and then reacted to point (K). Notice that the 60 point trailing INDEX SAR levels out after every new HIGH SWING POINT is made because the trailing stop is **always** measured from the most favorable ASI point. The 60 point trailing INDEX SAR is always a Stop and Reverse.

Point (K) is the first LOW SWING POINT after making a new HIGH SWING POINT. The ASI then moves up to (L), making a classic failure swing and then breaks below the INDEX SAR at (K) where we reverse and go *SHORT*. After going *SHORT*, the INDEX SAR is the previous HIGH SWING POINT at (L) because it is closer than the 60 point trailing INDEX SAR.

Now let's pick up the *SHORT* trade on Fig. 8.9. The ASI made a new LOW SWING POINT at (A). The **first** HIGH SWING POINT after making the new low is point (B), which becomes the SAR. Now watch what happens here. The ASI drops to point (D) then forms the **first** HIGH SWING POINT at (E). The ASI then drops straight down to point (F) and reacts straight up. Since no swing points were formed between (E) and (F), the 60 point ASI trailing stop becomes the closest INDEX SAR. We reverse to *LONG* at the trailing stop.

After making the new high for the trade at point (G), the **first** LOW SWING POINT is (H) which remains the INDEX SAR until the ASI makes a new HIGH SWING POINT and then the first LOW SWING POINT is formed. The INDEX SAR is then the **first** LOW SWING POINT after the new HIGH SWING POINT is made.

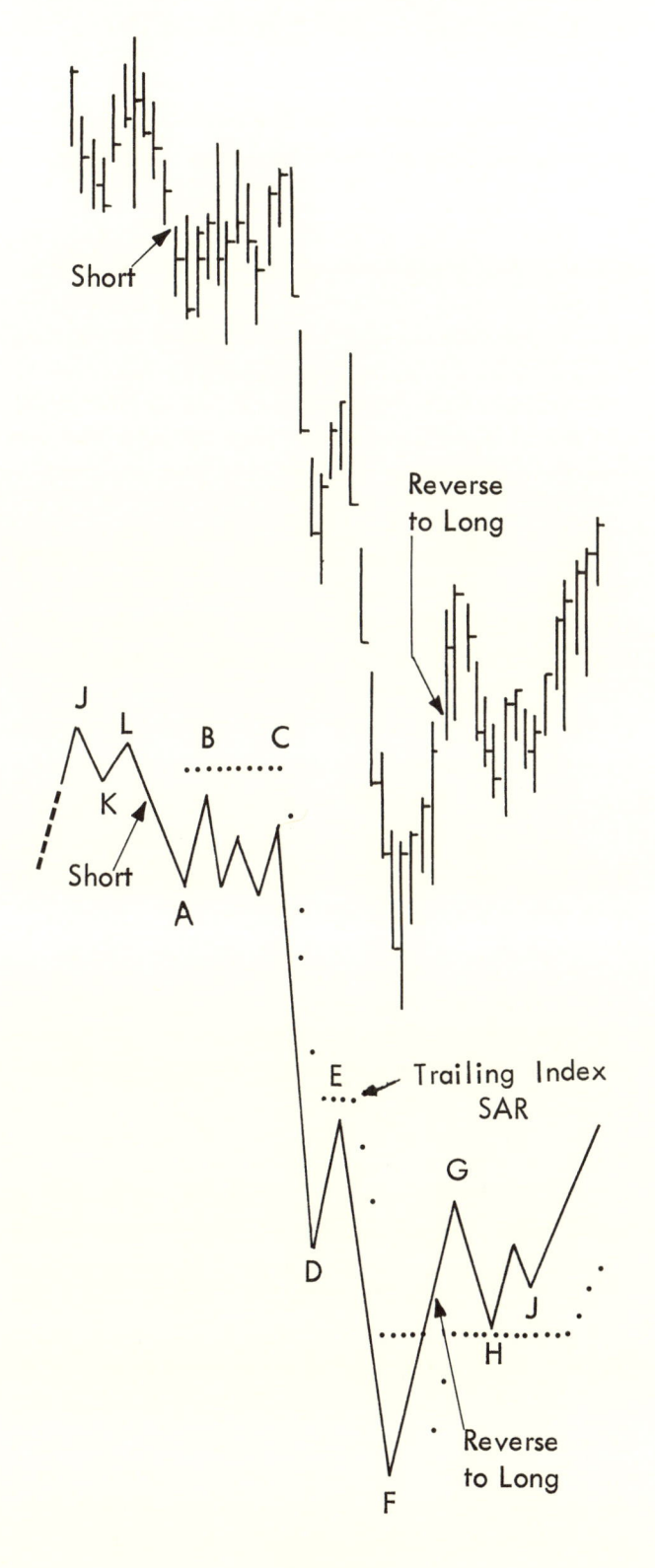

Fig. 8.9

I have explained this system by referring to LOW SWING POINTS and HIGH SWING POINTS for simplicity. **All** of the swing points are made by the ACCUMULATIVE SWING INDEX (ASI). In following this system on the work sheet, I have used the abbreviation LSP for LOW SWING POINT and HSP for HIGH SWING POINT. This abbreviation is put in the SI column beside the swing index value for the day the LSP and HSP is made. Of course, the swing point cannot be determined until the next day after it occurs.

Now that you understand the concept of this system, there is one thing left to define; that is, the relationship of the HSP, LSP and the INDEX SAR (made by the SWING INDEX) to the actual HIPS and LOPS (made by the price). We have to know which price points correspond to HSPs and LSPs and INDEX SARS in order to ascertain the exact market **price** to enter and exit the trade.

In effect, what we are really doing is **trading the line** which is made by connecting the AC-CUMULATIVE SWING INDEX points for each day. The ENTRY, EXIT and REVERSE signals **do not** come from price points directly; the **signals** come from the SWING INDEX points generated by the SI equation.

Once the signal has been made by the ASI, it is then necessary to translate the signal points into price action points.

The price action points which correspond to the HSPs and LSPs on the SWING INDEX are the HIPs and LOPs (as previously defined) which are made by the daily prices.

Remember, a HIP is a daily high price with a lower daily high price the day before it and the day after it. A LOP is a daily low price with a higher daily low price the day before it and the day after it.

Usually the HIP will occur on the same day as the HSP. In this case, the HIP is the SAR and is simply the highest price made on that day. If the lowest price occurs on the same day as the LSP, then the lowest price made that day, the LOP, is the SAR.

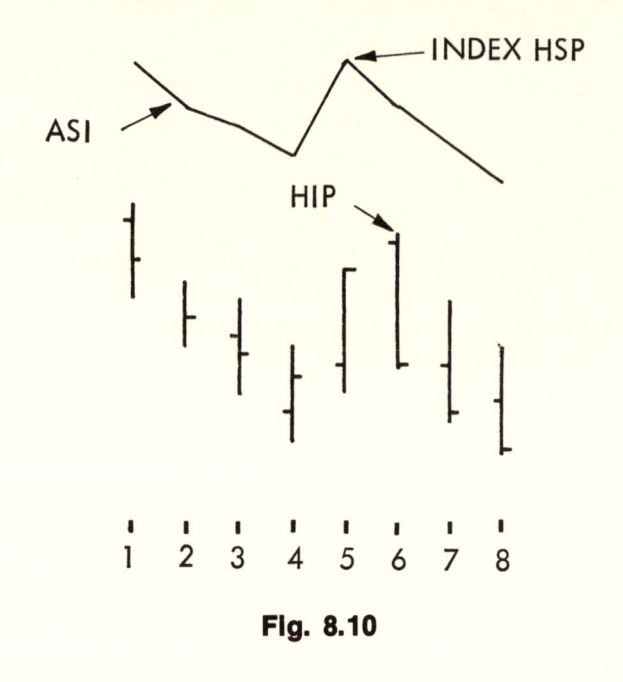

Fig. 8.10

In Fig. 8.10, the HSP occurred on Day 5; however, the HIP was made on Day 6. Although the **price** was higher on Day 6 than on Day 5, Day 6 will show up on the SWING INDEX as a minus (—) value . . . which it should . . . because it opened high, closed low, and also closed significantly lower than the previous day's close.

In Fig. 8.10, if we were *SHORT*, it is obvious that we would want to use the HIP on Day 6 as our SAR rather than the High on Day 5 which corresponds with the HSP.

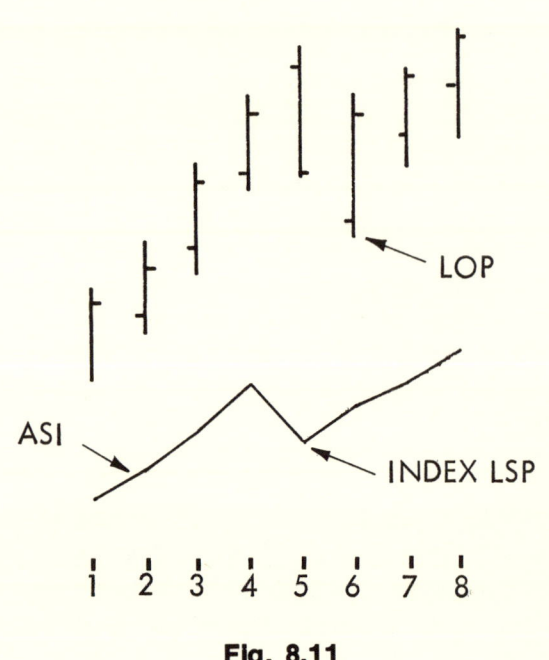

Fig. 8.11

In Fig. 8.11, the LOP is made on Day 6, but the LSP is made on Day 5. It is not unusual for the HSP and LSP to precede the HIP and LOP (made by the price) by one day.

In Fig. 8.11, if we were LONG, we would want to use the LOP made on Day 6 as our SAR even though the LSP occurred on Day 5.

As long as the HIP made by the price occurs on the same day as the HSP, then both the HIP and the HSP are recognized the next day after the high is made. However, suppose we are SHORT as in Fig. 8.10, and the market has closed on Day 6. The index HSP has formed, but we do not have a corresponding HIP. What SAR do we give our broker for Day 7? The answer is that we give him the high price made on Day 6. **We must assume that the HSP has preceded the HIP by one day.**

If we were LONG, as in Fig. 8.11, the same reasoning would apply to the LOP as shown. The SAR is the low price made on Day 6.

Now suppose our closest SAR is determined by the 60 point trailing INDEX SAR. Let's say that the market has closed and we calculate the ASI for the day and find that since the ASI high point was made, we have accumulated —65 points against the LONG position as illustrated in Fig. 8.12. What do we do? **We do not reverse on the open the next day.** We use the **lowest price** made since we began counting the 60 point drop on the ASI as our SAR. As will usually be the case, the SAR is the **low made today.**

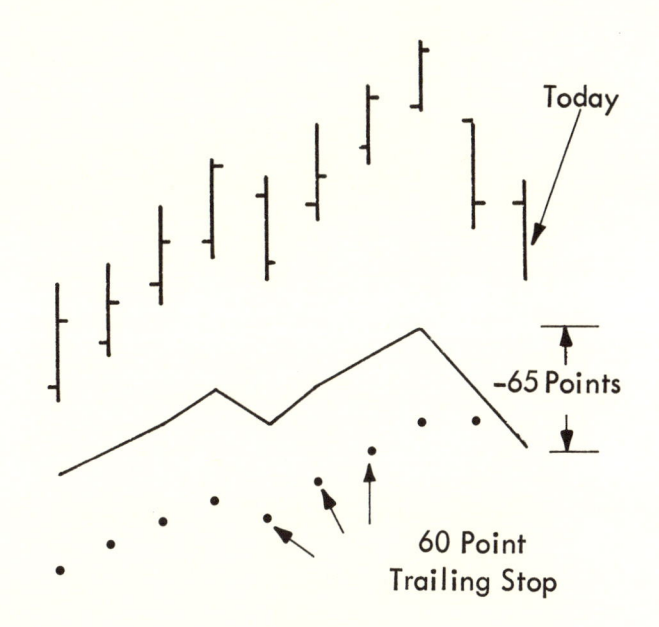

Fig. 8.12

In using this system, I have found that many times the price will turn around the next day and go to new highs without going through the low made on the day that —60 or more points was calculated. Also, I refrain from placing my order the next day until about five minutes after the open, if the price action is near my order. The first and last five minutes of trading are the most likely times for meaningless wide swings to pick off a stop order. Personally, I just don't like to give them something to "shoot at" on the open if my order is near the price action. Sometimes I even change a regular "stop" order to a "Stop on Close Only" order about 15 minutes before the close if the market action is near my order.

On the following pages are the definitions and rules for the SWING INDEX SYSTEM, which will be followed by a work sheet example and explanation.

DEFINITIONS

HSP	A HIGH SWING POINT is defined by the Accumulative Swing Index as any day with an ASI number that is higher than the ASI number the day before it and the day after it.
LSP	A LOW SWING POINT is defined by the Accumulative Swing Index as any day with an ASI number that is lower than the ASI number the day before it and the day after it.
SI	The SWING INDEX number generated by the Swing Index equation for a particular day.
ASI	The ACCUMULATIVE SWING INDEX number obtained for each day by adding or subtracting (as applicable) that day's SI number from the previous day's ASI number.
INDEX SAR	The STOP AND REVERSE points generated by the swing points of the **ASI**.
SAR	The STOP AND REVERSE points applicable to the **price**.
TRAILING INDEX SAR	An ASI number which is 60 ASI POINTS behind the most favorable ASI number while in the trade.

RULES
SWING INDEX SYSTEM

INITIAL ENTRY

    A. Enter *LONG* when the ASI crosses **above** the previous significant HSP.

    B. Enter *SHORT* when the ASI crosses **below** the previous significant LSP.

INDEX STOP AND REVERSE (SAR)

    A. *LONG:*   (1) Immediately after being reversed to *LONG* the SAR is the previous LSP.

                      (2) Thereafter, the SAR is the **first** LSP after a new HSP is made for the trade.

    B. *SHORT:*   (1) Immediately after being reversed to *SHORT,* the SAR is the previous HSP.

                      (2) Thereafter, the SAR is the **first** HSP after a new LSP is made for the trade.

INDEX
TRAILING STOP AND REVERSE (SAR)

    A. *LONG:*   The SAR is the **lowest daily low** made between the highest HSP and the close of the day on which the ASI decreased 60 points or more.

    B. *SHORT:*   The SAR is the **highest daily high** made between the lowest LSP and the close of the day on which the ASI increased 60 points or more.

Note: *The RULES are given in accordance with the ACCUMULATIVE SWING INDEX **only**, and **must** be correlated with the PRICE ACTION POINTS as explained in the text.*

SWING INDEX SYSTEM — WORK SHEET EXAMPLE

Day 10   The previous significant HSP was 104 (Col. #13) made on Day 6. The HIP of 46.00 was also made on Day 6. On Day 10, the ASI exceeded 104 for the first time. We therefore entered an order on Day 11 to Buy at 46.05 (a tick or two above 46.00). The entry stop point is 43.00, which is the LOP, the lowest low price which corresponds to the previous LSP made on Day 7.

Day 14   The **first** LSP was formed after a new high of 133 on the ASI. Note that the LSP made by the ASI occurred on the same day as the LOP made by the price. On Day 14, the SAR therefore is the low of 45.00 made on Day 13. From there, the price moved straight up to 61.80 on Day 19.

Day 20   The ASI has backed up a total of 64 points without making an LSP after the ASI high of 459, thus triggering the trailing INDEX SAR. The lowest low price made between the highest ASI (while in the trade) and the close on Day 20 is, as usual, the **low** on Day 20. We therefore enter our SAR on Day 21 of 56.45 which is a tick or two below the lowest low.

Day 21   Our SAR at 56.45 is touched off and we are *SHORT* at 56.45. Our new SAR, the previous HSP, is the HIP made on Day 19 at 61.80.

Day 23   An HSP is identified as having occurred on Day 22. The HIP, however, is not recognized on Day 23. We therefore assume the HSP preceded the HIP by one day so we use the HIP made on Day 23 as our SAR. The HSP on Day 20 is the **first** HSP after a new LSP was made by the ASI on Day 21. The SAR is now 57.50 plus a tick or two.

Day 27   The ASI made a new low, 340, on Day 25 and the first HSP is now identified as having occurred on Day 26. The HIP of 55.00 is the same for Days 26 and 27, so 55.00 becomes the new SAR.

Day 28   The price went through our SAR and we are *LONG* at 55.05. Our new SAR is the LOP corresponding to the previous LSP made on Day 27. The SAR is therefore 53.00.

Day 31   After making a new high for the trade, 447 HSP on Day 29, the first LSP was identified on Day 31. The SAR which corresponds to the LSP is 59.00.

Day 32   We are *SHORT* at 58.95. The SAR which corresponds to the previous HSP is 61.50.

Day 35   The ASI made a new low for the trade, 383, on Day 33 and then swung up and made the **first** HSP on Day 34 at 385. This HSP is identified on Day 35 and the corresponding SAR is 58.50.

Day 39   The ASI made a new low for the trade, 257, on Day 36. The **first** HSP is now recognized at 310, made on Day 38.

Day 41   An HSP is identified as having occurred on Day 40; however, since it was not preceded by a new ASI low for the trade, the SAR remains at 55.00.

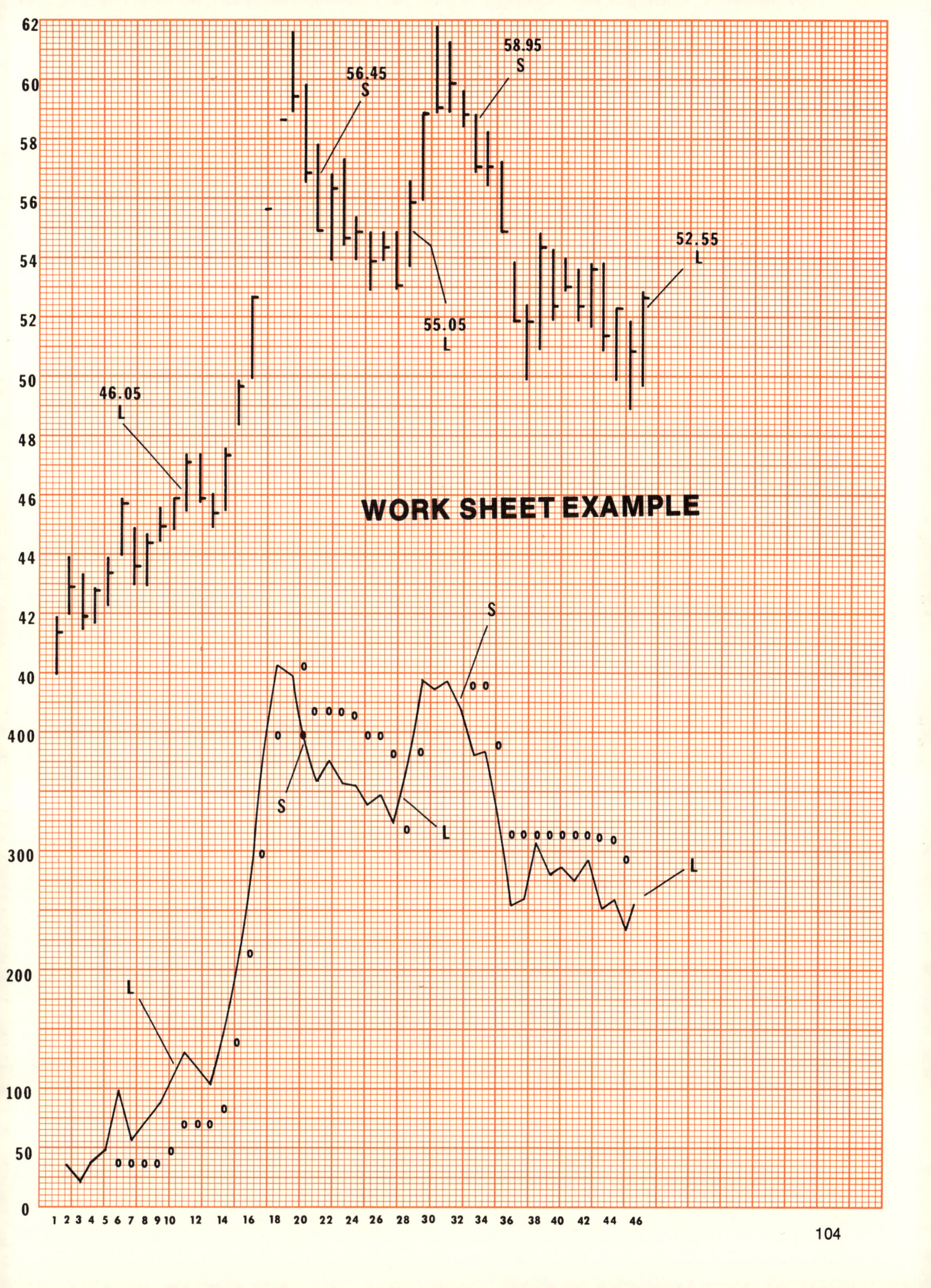

WORK SHEET EXAMPLE

DAILY WORK SHEET
SWING INDEX SYSTEM

					USE ABSOLUTE VALUE				USE + OR − VALUE			
DATE	OPEN	HIGH	LOW	CLOSE	(1) H_2-C_1	(2) L_2-C_1	(3) H_2-L_2	(4) C_1-O_1	(5) C_2-C_1	(6) C_2-O_2	(7) C_1-O_1	(8) N
1	40.50	42.00	40.00	41.50								
2	42.00	44.00	42.00	43.00	2.50	.50	2.00	1.00	1.50	1.00	1.00	2.25
3	42.80	43.50	41.50	42.00	.50	1.50	2.00	1.00	-1.00	-.80	1.00	-1.15
4	41.70	43.00	41.70	42.90								
5	43.00	44.00	42.30	43.50								
6	44.50	(46.00)	44.00	45.80								
7	44.80	45.00	(43.00)	43.50								
8	43.00	44.80	(43.00)	44.50								
9	44.70	45.70	44.50	45.00	1.20	0	1.20	1.50	.50	.30	1.50	1.03
10	45.00	46.00	44.90	46.00	1.00	.10	1.10	0	1.00	1.00	.30	1.58
11	45.80	47.50	45.50	47.20	1.50	.50	2.00	1.00	1.20	1.40	1.00	2.15
12	47.00	47.50	45.80	46.00	.30	1.40	1.70	1.40	-1.20	-1.00	1.40	-1.35
13	46.20	46.20	(45.00)	45.50	.20	1.00	1.20	1.00	-1.00	-.70	-1.00	-1.10
14	45.80	47.70	45.50	47.50	2.20	0	2.20	.70	2.00	1.70	-.70	2.67
15	48.50	50.00	48.40	49.80	2.50	.90	1.60	1.70	2.30	1.30	1.70	3.38
16	50.00	52.80	50.00	52.80	3.00	.20	2.80	1.30	3.00	2.80	1.30	4.73
17	55.80	55.80	55.80	55.80	3.00	3.00	0	2.80	3.00	0	2.80	3.70
18	58.80	58.80	58.80	58.80	3.00	3.00	0	0	3.00	0	0	3.00
19	61.80	(61.80)	59.00	59.50	3.00	.20	2.80	0	.70	-2.30	0	-.45
20	60.00	60.00	(56.50)	57.00	.50	3.00	3.50	2.30	-2.50	-3.00	-2.30	-4.58
21	57.50	58.00	55.00	55.00	1.00	2.00	3.00	3.00	-2.00	-2.50	-3.00	-4.00
22	54.00	57.00	54.00	56.50	2.00	1.00	3.00	2.50	1.50	2.50	-2.50	2.12
23	57.00	(57.50)	54.70	54.80	1.00	2.00	3.00	2.50	-1.70	-2.20	2.50	-2.17
24	54.50	55.50	54.00	55.00	.70	.80	1.50	2.20	.20	.50	-2.20	-.10
25	54.50	(55.00)	53.00	54.00	0	2.00	2.00	.50	-1.00	-.50	.50	-1.12
26	54.00	55.00	54.00	54.50	1.00	0	1.00	.50	.50	.50	-.50	.62
27	55.00	55.00	(53.00)	53.20	.50	1.50	2.00	.50	-1.30	-1.80	.50	-2.07
28	53.80	56.80	53.80	56.00	3.60	.60	3.00	1.80	2.80	2.20	-1.80	3.45
29	56.50	59.00	56.00	59.00	3.00	0	3.00	2.20	3.00	2.50	2.20	4.80
30	62.00	62.00	(59.00)	59.20	3.00	0	3.00	2.52	.20	2.80	2.52	-.57
31	59.50	(61.50)	59.00	60.00	2.30	.20	2.50	2.80	.80	.50	-2.80	.35
32	59.50	59.80	58.50	59.00	.20	1.50	1.30	.50	-1.00	-.50	.50	-1.12
33	58.50	59.00	57.00	57.20	0	2.00	2.00	.50	-1.80	-1.30	-.50	-2.58
34	57.00	(58.50)	56.50	57.50	1.30	.70	2.00	1.30	.30	.50	-1.30	.22
35	57.00	57.50	55.00	55.00	0	2.50	2.50	.50	-2.50	-2.00	.50	-3.37
36	54.00	54.00	52.00	52.00	1.00	3.00	2.00	2.00	-3.00	-2.00	-2.00	-4.50
37	50.00	52.50	50.00	52.00	.50	2.00	2.50	2.00	0	2.00	-2.00	.50
38	52.00	(55.00)	51.00	54.50	3.00	1.00	4.00	2.00	2.50	2.50	2.00	4.25
39	54.00	54.50	52.00	52.50	0	2.50	2.50	2.50	-2.00	-1.50	2.50	-2.12
40	53.00	54.20	53.00	53.20	1.70	.50	1.20	1.50	.70	.20	-1.50	.42
41	53.50	53.80	52.00	52.50	.60	1.20	1.80	.20	-.70	-1.00	.20	-1.15
42	52.00	54.00	51.80	53.80	1.50	.70	2.20	1.00	1.30	1.80	-1.00	1.95
43	54.00	54.00	51.00	51.50	.20	2.80	3.00	1.80	-2.30	-2.50	1.80	3.10
44	51.00	(52.50)	50.00	52.50	1.00	1.50	2.50	2.50	2.50	1.50	-2.50	1.12
45	52.00	52.00	(49.00)	51.00	.50	3.50	3.00	1.50	-1.50	-1.00	1.50	-1.62
46	51.00	53.00	49.80	52.80	2.00	1.20	3.20	1.00	1.80	1.80	-1.00	2.45
47	52.40	54.20	52.00	54.00	1.40	.80	2.20	1.80	1.20	1.60	1.80	2.45

Col 8 = (5) + ½ (6) + ¼ (7)
Col 9 = larger of (1) or (2)

If (1) largest col 10 = (1) − ½ (2) + ¼ (4)
If (2) largest col 10 = (2) − ½ (1) + ¼ (4)
If (3) largest col 10 = (3) + ¼ (4)

Col 11 = limit
Col 12 = 50 × (8) ÷ (10) × (9) ÷ (11)

COMMODITY _____

CONTRACT MONTH _____

(9) K	(10) R	(11) L	(12) SI	(13) ASI	SAR	ACTION and ORDER
2.50	2.50	3.00	37	37		
1.50	2.25	3.00	−13 LSP	24		
			15	39		
			11	50		
			54 HSP	(104)		
			−45 LSP	59		
			15	74		
1.20	1.58		13	87		
1.00	1.18		22	109		
1.50	2.25		24 HSP	133	43.00	L−46.05
1.40	2.05		−16	117		
1.00	1.45		−13 LSP	(104)		
2.20	2.38		41	145	45.00	
2.50	2.48		57	202		
3.00	3.23		73	275		
3.00	2.20		84	359		
3.00	1.50		100 HSP	459		
3.00	2.90		−8	451		
3.00	4.08	−64	−56	395	56.50	Accum
2.00	3.75		−36 LSP	359	61.80	S−56.45 +10.40
2.00	3.63		20 HSP	379		
2.00	3.63		−20	359	57.50	
.80	2.05		−1	358		
2.00	2.13		−18 LSP	340		
1.00	1.13		9 HSP	(349)		
1.50	2.13		−25 LSP	324	55.00	
3.60	3.75		55	379	53.00	L−55.05 +1.40 +11.80
3.00	3.55		68 HSP	447		
3.00	3.63		−8 LSP	439		
2.30	3.20		4 HSP	(443)	59.00	
1.50	1.53		−19	424	61.50	S−58.95 +3.90 +15.70
2.00	2.13		−4 LSP	383		
1.30	2.33		2 HSP	(385)		
2.50	2.63		−53	332	58.50	
3.00	3.00		−75 LSP	257		
2.00	3.00		6	263		
3.00	4.50		47 HSP	(310)		
2.50	3.13		−28 LSP	282	55.00	
1.70	1.83		7 HSP	(289)		
1.20	1.85		−13 LSP	276		
1.50	2.45		20 HSP	296		
2.80	3.45		−42 LSP	254		
1.50	3.13		9 HSP	(263)		
3.50	3.62		−27 LSP	236	52.50	
2.00	3.45		24	260	49.00	L−52.53 +6.40 +22.10
1.40	2.65		22	282		

Day 42   The ASI at 296 goes above the previous HSP of 289. However, we do not take action until or if the ASI breaks the **first** upswing after the 257 low which is 310.

Day 45   The ASI made a new low for the trade of 254 on Day 43. The **first** upswing after the new low is confirmed on Day 45. The SAR is the HIP on Day 44 of 52.50.

Day 46   We went *LONG* at 52.55. The new SAR is the LOP of 49.00 corresponding to the previous LSP made on Day 45.

This system performs best on those entities which are high on the Average Directional Movement Index Rating (ADXR). One option that can be used with this system is to simply stop trading after two consecutive loss trades and then use the initial entry procedure for the next trade.

The following chart shows the system trading Cocoa for one full year.

Cocoa (Swing System)

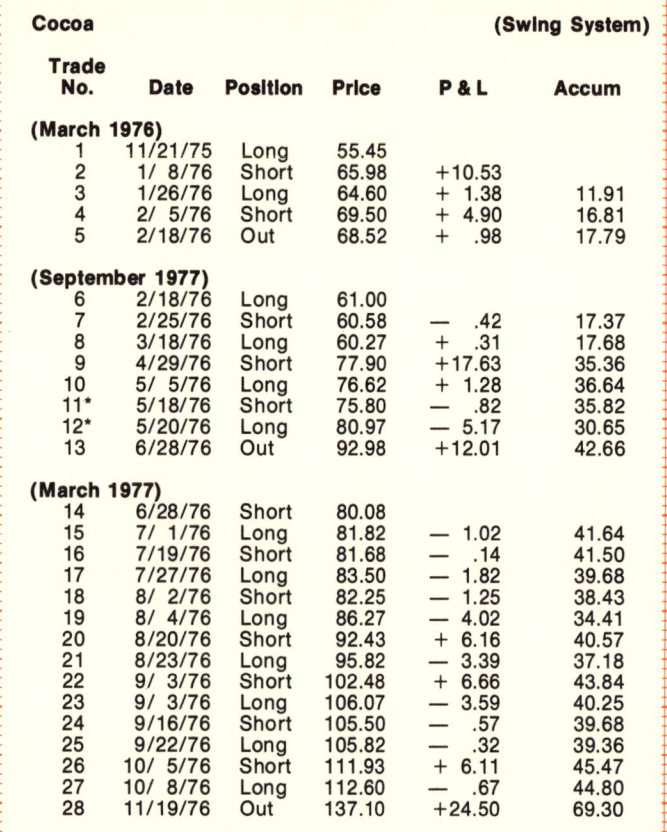

Trade No.	Date	Position	Price	P & L	Accum
(March 1976)					
1	11/21/75	Long	55.45		
2	1/ 8/76	Short	65.98	+10.53	
3	1/26/76	Long	64.60	+ 1.38	11.91
4	2/ 5/76	Short	69.50	+ 4.90	16.81
5	2/18/76	Out	68.52	+ .98	17.79
(September 1977)					
6	2/18/76	Long	61.00		
7	2/25/76	Short	60.58	— .42	17.37
8	3/18/76	Long	60.27	+ .31	17.68
9	4/29/76	Short	77.90	+17.63	35.36
10	5/ 5/76	Long	76.62	+ 1.28	36.64
11*	5/18/76	Short	75.80	— .82	35.82
12*	5/20/76	Long	80.97	— 5.17	30.65
13	6/28/76	Out	92.98	+12.01	42.66
(March 1977)					
14	6/28/76	Short	80.08		
15	7/ 1/76	Long	81.82	— 1.02	41.64
16	7/19/76	Short	81.68	— .14	41.50
17	7/27/76	Long	83.50	— 1.82	39.68
18	8/ 2/76	Short	82.25	— 1.25	38.43
19	8/ 4/76	Long	86.27	— 4.02	34.41
20	8/20/76	Short	92.43	+ 6.16	40.57
21	8/23/76	Long	95.82	— 3.39	37.18
22	9/ 3/76	Short	102.48	+ 6.66	43.84
23	9/ 3/76	Long	106.07	— 3.59	40.25
24	9/16/76	Short	105.50	— .57	39.68
25	9/22/76	Long	105.82	— .32	39.36
26	10/ 5/76	Short	111.93	+ 6.11	45.47
27	10/ 8/76	Long	112.60	— .67	44.80
28	11/19/76	Out	137.10	+24.50	69.30

*Not shown due to lack of space.

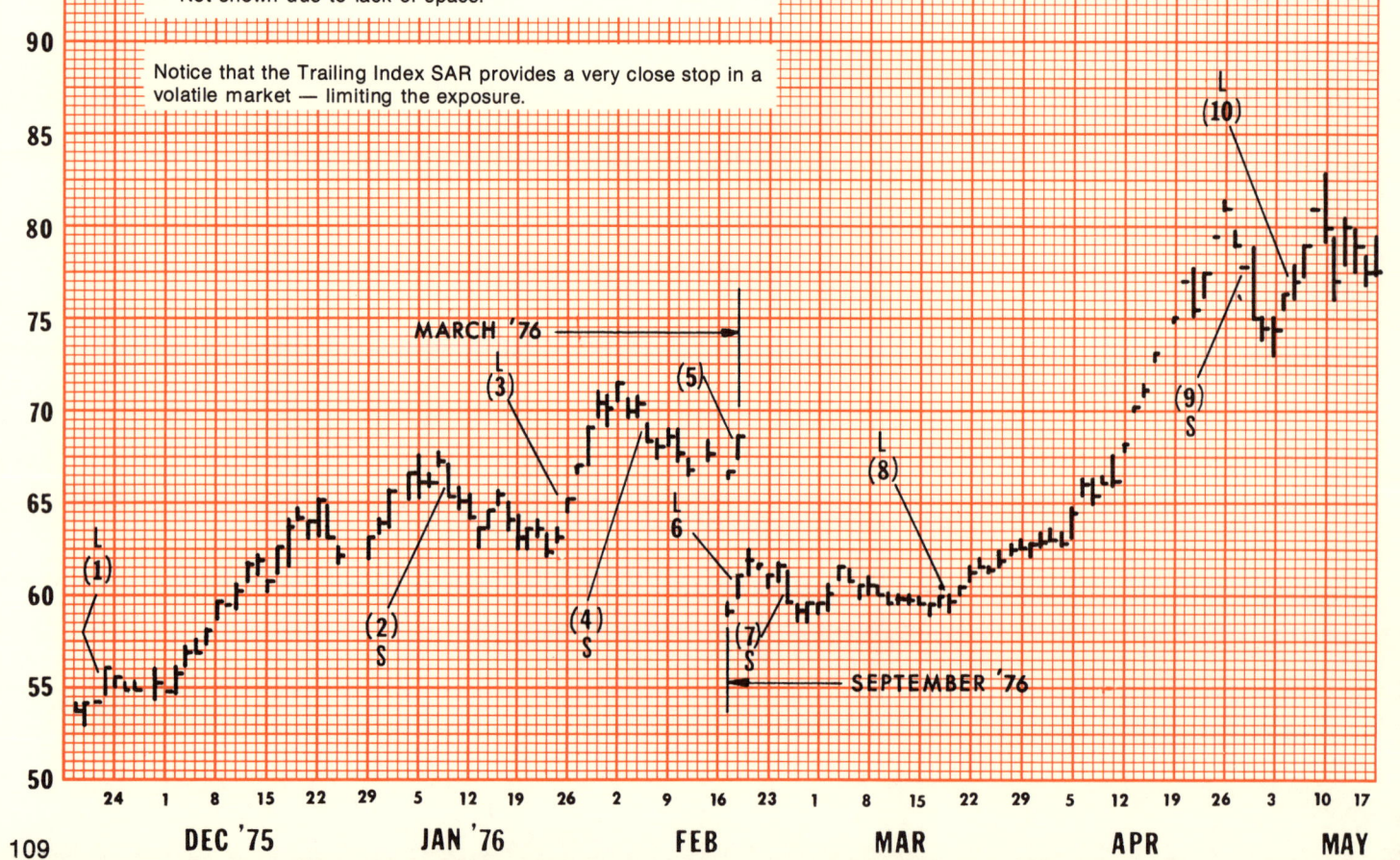

Notice that the Trailing Index SAR provides a very close stop in a volatile market — limiting the exposure.

109

SEPTEMBER '76
MARCH '77
(13)
OUT
L
(15)
(14)
S
(16)
S
L
(17)
L
(19)
(18)
S
L
(21)
(20)
S
L
(23)
(22)
S
L
(25)
(24)
S
L
(27)
(26)
S
(28)
OUT
145
140
135
130
125
120
115
110
105
100
95
90
85
80
75
70
65
60
55
31
7
14
21
28
5
12
19
26
2
9
16
23
30
6
13
20
27
4
11
18
25
1
8
15
JUN
JULY
AUG
SEPT
OCT
NOV

SECTION IX

THE COMMODITY SELECTION INDEX

From Section III, we learned how to rate the commodities or stocks being followed as to which are the most VOLATILE.

In Section IV, we learned how to rate the same entities relative to their DIRECTIONAL MOVEMENT.

Volatility is also an indicator of movement. The paradox is that volatility is always accompanied by movement, but movement is not always accompanied by volatility. A commodity can move up very slowly and be high on the Average Directional Movement Index Rating (ADXR) but still be low on the Volatility Index.

For this reason, the most important index to use for a trend-following system is the ADXR; however, generally the most money is made in the shortest period of time when the stock or commodity is volatile. For those who don't like the risk associated with volatile markets, they should stay with the ADXR and trade the commodities on the higher end of the scale which suit their inclinations and pocketbooks.

For those who have the capital and are looking for the best overall situation, then the Commodity Selection Index (CSI) equation takes in all of the following factors:

(1) Directional Movement
(2) Volatility
(3) Margin Requirement
(4) Commission costs

The factors are individually weighted in the order listed above. Here is the COMMODITY SELECTION INDEX EQUATION.

$$CSI = ADXR \times ATR_{14} \left[\frac{V}{\sqrt{M}} \times \frac{1}{150 + C} \right] 100$$

Where   ADXR = Average Directional Movement Index Rating

ATR_{14} = 14-Day Average True Range

V = Value of a 1¢ move (or the basic increment of the ATR_{14} in Dollars)

M = Margin Requirement in Dollars $\sqrt{M}$ = Square root of M

C = Commission in Dollars

NOTE: the result of the term $\dfrac{1}{150 + C}$ must be carried to **four** decimal places

Now let's look at an example. Suppose the factors for two commodities are as follows:

	ADXR	ATR$_{14}$	M	C	V
Soybeans	50	15¢	$3000	$45	$ 50
Pork Bellies	37	1.7¢	$1500	$60	$360

Substituting in the equation for **Soybeans:**

$$\text{CSI} = 50 \times 15.00 \left[\dfrac{50}{\sqrt{3000}} \times \dfrac{1}{150 + 45} \right] 100$$

$$= 50 \times 15.00 \left[\dfrac{50}{54.77} \times \dfrac{1}{195} \right] 100$$

$$= 50 \times 15.00 \quad \times .91 \quad \times \quad .0051 \quad \times 100$$

$$= 348 \text{ (for Soybeans)}$$

Substituting in the equation for **Pork Bellies:**

$$\text{CSI} = 37 \times 1.70 \left[\dfrac{360}{\sqrt{1500}} \times \dfrac{1}{150 + 60} \right] 100$$

$$= 37 \times 1.70 \left[\dfrac{360}{38.73} \times \dfrac{1}{210} \right] 100$$

$$= 37 \times 1.70 \quad \times 9.30 \quad \times \quad .0048 \quad \times 100$$

$$= 280 \text{ (for Pork Bellies)}$$

Therefore, Soybeans has the higher rating of the two.

Now let's look again at the CSI equation and point out a short cut that can be used:

All the values inside the brackets are **constant** as long as the margin requirement and the commission cost do not change. The 100 is also a constant.

The equation then, can be rewritten so that "K" represents all of the constants:

$$\text{CSI} = \text{ADXR} \times \text{ATR}_{14} \times K$$

We can therefore calculate "K" one time for each commodity being followed and use that value every day multiplied times the ADXR and the ATR$_{14}$ to obtain the CSI for that day. We only have to recalculate K when and if either the margin requirement changes or the commission rate changes.

In the previous CSI equation for **Soybeans**:

$$\text{CSI} = 50 \times 15.00 \left[\dfrac{50}{\sqrt{3000}} \times \dfrac{1}{150 + 45} \right] 100$$

$$K = \left[\frac{50}{\sqrt{3000}} \times \frac{1}{150 + 45}\right] 100$$

$$= .91 \times .0051 \times 100$$

$$= .4641$$

Therefore, CSI = ADXR × ATR$_{14}$ × K
= 50 × 15 × .4641
= 348

For **Bellies:**

$$K = \left[\frac{360}{\sqrt{1500}} \times \frac{1}{150 + 60}\right] 100$$

$$= 9.30 \times .0048 \times 100$$

$$= 4.464$$

Therefore, CSI = ADXR × ATR$_{14}$ × K
= 37 × 1.70 × 4.464
= 280

The last three columns on the **Directional Movement Index** work sheet are entitled ADXR, ATR$_{14}$ and CSI. Just above the three columns is a space for K. The CSI can be calculated daily by using K and the values already obtained for the Directional Movement Index work sheet.

The ADXR is the latest ADX plus the ADX 14 days ago, divided by 2, as explained in the section on DIRECTIONAL MOVEMENT.

The ATR$_{14}$ is the value in the ATR column divided by 14.

To obtain the CSI for each day, simply multiply ADXR × ATR$_{14}$ × K and insert the value in the CSI column.

Now let's look at an extreme example. Suppose Coffee is highest on the ADXR at 70 and the Volatility Index shows that its Average True Range (ATR$_{14}$) is 3.75¢.

At $375.00 for a 1¢ move, the average dollar movement per day is 3.75 × 375 = $1,406.25. Sounds good so far, but if the margin requirement is $9,000 per contract and the commission is $85.00, then how does Coffee compare with trading Soybeans in the previous example? The factors are as follows:

	ADXR	ATR$_{14}$	M	C	V
Soybeans	50	15¢	$3000	$45	$ 50
Coffee	70	3.75¢	$9000	$85	$375

For Coffee:

$$\text{CSI} = 70 \times 3.75 \left[\frac{375}{\sqrt{9000}} \times \frac{1}{150 + 85} \right] 100$$

$$= 70 \times 3.75 \left[\frac{375}{94.87} \times \frac{1}{235} \right] 100$$

$$= 70 \times 3.75 \times 3.95 \times .0043 \times 100$$

$$= 318 \text{ (for Coffee)}$$

The CSI for Soybeans was 348; therefore, Soybeans is the better overall deal. Now let's analyze the Soybean situation:

The Average True Range (ATR_{14}) is 15¢ x 50.00 = $750 average dollar movement per day. This is only about half that of Coffee, and in addition, Soybeans has less directional movement than Coffee.

To give you an idea of what the CSI equation does, let's make two general suppositions; let's say that we traded both Coffee and Soybeans:

(1) Suppose we got 70% of the move in Coffee since ADXR for Coffee was 70, the same reasoning would give us 50% of the Soybean move.
(2) Suppose we are in each trade for ten days, so that our money is tied up for the same period of time.

For Coffee:

$1,406.25 per day for ten days x 70% =	$9,843.75
Less commission	85.00
Profit	$9,758.75

For Soybeans:

$750 per day for ten days x 50% =	$3,750.00
Less commission	45.00
Profit	$3,705.00

However, due to the difference in margin requirement, we could have traded **three** contracts of Soybeans for **each** contract of Coffee; therefore, 3 x $3,705 = $11,115.

The profit on Soybeans was	$11,115.00
The profit on Coffee was	9,758.75

The COMMODITY SELECTION INDEX for Soybeans was 348
The COMMODITY SELECTION INDEX for Coffee was 318

$$30 \div 318 = 9\%$$

NEW CONCEPTS IN TECHNICAL TRADING SYSTEMS

The ADXR indicated that Soybeans was a 9% better deal than Coffee. Actually, in the example Soybeans was a 13.9% better deal than Coffee.

$$\begin{array}{r} \$11{,}115.00 \\ -9{,}758.75 \\ \hline \$1{,}356.25 \div 9758.75 = 13.9\% \end{array}$$

I realize that what we are dealing with here is not an exact science. The margin requirements will not be set, nor could they be set to maintain a constant relationship with volatility or directional movement, nor any other variable, for that matter. There is, however, a direct — though not constant — relationship between margin requirement, volatility and directional movement. The CSI equation constantly analyzes all of these factors and points out the most advantageous situations.

As a rule, margin requirements lag market action. They are slow to go up and slow to go down. The COMMODITY SELECTION INDEX also enables the trader to take advantage of this lag to obtain the best return on invested capital.

Most technical systems are trend-following systems; however, most commodities are in a good trending mode (high directional movement) only about 30% of the time. **If the trader follows the same commodities or stocks all of the time, then his system has to be good enough to make more money 30% of the time than it will give back 70% of the time. Compare that approach to trading only the top five or six commodities on the CSI scale. This is the underlying concept . . . the reason this book was written.**

SECTION X

CAPITAL MANAGEMENT

The message of this book is that there are three parts to a good technical trading plan:

(1) Using a good technical system.
(2) Using the system on the right market(s) at the right time.
(3) Using a good money management technique.

Of these three, the third is the most important, the easiest to learn . . . and the hardest to do.

It is the hardest to do because at one time or another, most of us have put all our marbles in one basket, timed it just right, and made a tremendous profit. When this happens, the results are usually two-fold. One, it boosts our ego and confidence to the point that we think we can do it at least one more time; second, the profit was made so quickly that we don't consider it in the same light as if it took us several years to earn it.

One of the smartest businessmen I know started out with a horse, a homemade sawmill and a fourth grade education. Over the years, he became a multimillionaire, dealing in land and timber. He made a statement that I have never forgotten. He said, "Boys, when you really make a big profit fast, you have got to get **used** to having it. Don't do anything with it for six months. By that time, you will be **used** to having it and you will treat it prudently."

This man had learned something that many of us never learn.

I can sum up my concept of money management in two sentences:

(1) Don't margin more than 15% of total capital on any one commodity.
(2) Don't margin more than 60% of total capital at any one time.

These are the limits. I prefer to trade the six top commodities on the CSI scale with not over 10% of total capital on any one commodity. I use this criteria on my own account and on the accounts which I manage.

There is one more concept I would like to leave with you. This is not new — it was old when the Phoenicians were trading with the Romans and the Greek Philosophers cornered the olive oil market. The concept is this . . .

The percent gain it takes to recover a loss increases geometrically with the loss. For example, if we lose 15% of our capital, we have to make 17.6% gain on the balance to get even. However, if we lose 30% of our capital, it will take 42.9% gain on the balance we have left to get even; and if we lose 50% of our capital, it will take 100% gain on the balance to get even.

This concept is set out in the little table which follows. I have a copy of this table posted on the wall near my desk as a reminder of the importance of capital management.

% Loss of Initial Capital	% Gain on Balance Required to Recover
5	5.3
10	11.1
15	17.6
20	25.0
25	33.3
30	42.9
35	53.8
40	66.7
45	81.8
50	100.0
55	122.0
60	150.0
65	186.0
70	233.0
75	300.0
80	400.0
85	567.0
90	900.0

CONCLUSION

At the beginning of this book, I made the statement that I had never seen a technical trading system that **consistently** makes profits in ALL markets. Trend-following systems can make consistent profits in a **directional** market and consistent losses in a **non-directional** market. The answer, therefore, is to discover a way to define directional movement and translate this definition to a rating scale within known parameters.

The DIRECTIONAL MOVEMENT INDEX (Average Directional Movement Index Rating ADXR) is my answer to this problem. The ADXR may not be the best answer, nor may it be the final answer; but to my knowledge, it is the first truly definitive answer.

Several times in the past, I have come to the conclusion after perfecting and testing a system that it was the 'ultimate' method. I would decide to stop searching and researching and be content to just trade the system . . . and then . . . as I did this morning, I will awake about 3 o'clock a.m., with another new concept to explore. It seems to be a never-ending search.

Perhaps if the early morning Revelations continue, someday there will be NEW CONCEPTS IN TECHNICAL TRADING SYSTEMS — BOOK II.

Good luck and good trading.

APPENDIX

GLOSSARY OF TERMS AND ABBREVIATIONS

ABS	Absolute value
ADX	Average Directional Movement Index
ADXR	Average Directional Movement Index Rating
AF	Acceleration Factor
ARC	Average Range times Constant
ATR	Average True Range
B_1	Buy Point
C	Close
CSI	Commodity Selection Index
DIFF	Difference between two prices
$+DI_1$	UP directional indicator for one day
$-DI_1$	DOWN directional indicator for one day
$+DI_{14}$	Sum of $+DI_1$ for 14 days
$-DI_{14}$	Sum of $-DI_1$ for 14 days
$+DM_1$	UP directional movement for one day
$-DM_1$	DOWN directional movement for one day
$+DM_{14}$	Sum of $+DM_1$ for 14 days
$-DM_{14}$	Sum of $-DM_1$ for 14 days
DX	Directional Movement Index
EP	Extreme Price
H	High
HBOP	High Break Out Point
HIP	High Point
HI SIP	Significant High Point
HSP	High Swing Point
K	Constant
L	Low
LBOP	Low Break Out Point
LOP	Low Point
LO SIP	Significant Low Point
LSP	Low Swing Point
MF	Momentum Factor
O	Open
RS	Relative Strength
RSI	Relative Strength Index
S_1	Sell Point
SAR	Stop and Reverse Point
SI	Swing Index
SIC	Significant Close
SIP	Significant Point
TBP	Trend Balance Point
TR_1	Today's True Range
TR_{14}	Sum of TR_1 for 14 days
VI	Volatility Index
X	Average of the High, Low and Close Price for one day

DAILY WORK SHEET

PARABOLIC TIME / PRICE SYSTEM

DATE	OPEN	HIGH	LOW	CLOSE	SAR (1)	EP (2)	EP±SAR (3)	AF (4)	AF X DIFF (5)

COMMODITY _____ CONTRACT MONTH _____

NTRY	EXIT	P & L	ACTION and ORDER

DAILY WORK SHEET
VOLATILITY SYSTEM

COMMODITY _____   CONTRACT MONTH _____

DATE	OPEN	HIGH	LOW	CLOSE	TR_1	ATR	ARC	SAR	ACTION and ORDER

DAILY WORK SHEET

RELATIVE STRENGTH INDEX

COMMODITY _____

CONTRACT MONTH _____

(1) DATE	(2) CLOSE	(3) UP	(4) DOWN	(5) UP AVG	(6) DOWN AVG	(7) (5) ÷ (6)	(8) 1 + (7)	(9) 100 ÷ (8)	(10) 100 − (9)

DAILY WORK SHEET

DIRECTIONAL MOVEMENT INDEX

(1) DATE	(2) OPEN	(3) HIGH	(4) LOW	(5) CLOSE	(6) TR 1	(7) +DM 1	(8) −DM 1	(9) TR 14	(10) +DM 14	(11) −DM 14	(12) +DI 14 [(10)÷(9)]	(13) −DI 14 [(11)÷(9)]

COMMODITY _____ CONTRACT MONTH _____

K _____

)−(13)	(12)+(13)	(14)÷(15)	(17)	ACTION and ORDER	ADXR	ATR 14	CSI
14) DIFF	(15) DI SUM	(16) DX	ADX				

130

DAILY WORK SHEET

TREND BALANCE POINT SYSTEM

DATE	OPEN	HIGH	LOW	CLOSE	MF	TR	$\bar{X}$	TBP	$\bar{X}$ - TR LG STOP

| DATE | OPEN | HIGH | LOW | CLOSE | MF | TR | $\bar{X}$ | TBP | $\bar{X}$ - TR LG STOP |

COMMODITY _____ CONTRACT MONTH _____

$\overline{X}-L$ TARGET	$\overline{X}+TR$ ST STOP	$2\overline{X}-H$ ST TARGET	ENTRY	EXIT	ACTION and ORDER

DAILY WORK SHEET
THE REACTION TREND SYSTEM

DATE	OPEN	HIGH	LOW	CLOSE	$\bar{X}$	$2\bar{X}-H$ B_1	$2\bar{X}-L$ S_1	$2\bar{X}-2L+H$ HBOP	$2\bar{X}-2H+L$ LBOP

COMMODITY _____ CONTRACT MONTH _____

ENTRY	EXIT	P&L	ACTION and ORDER

DAILY WORK SHEET
SWING INDEX SYSTEM

DATE	OPEN	HIGH	LOW	CLOSE	(1) H_2-C_1	(2) L_2-C_1	(3) H_2-L_2	(4) C_1-O_1	(5) C_2-C_1	(6) C_2-O_2	(7) C_1-O_1	(8) N

← USE ABSOLUTE VALUE → ← USE + OR − VALUE →

Col 8 = (5) + ½ (6) + ¼ (7)
Col 9 = larger of (1) or (2)

COMMODITY _____

CONTRACT MONTH _____

f (1) largest col 10 = (1) − ½ (2) + ¼ (4)
f (2) largest col 10 = (2) − ½ (1) + ¼ (4)
f (3) largest col 10 = (3)   + ¼ (4)

Col 11 = limit
Col 12 = 50 × (8) ÷ (10) × (9) ÷ (11)

(9) K	(10) R	(11) L	(12) SI	(13) ASI	SAR	ACTION and ORDER